Praise for *We C*
Bible with the P

"Rev. Dr. Liz Theoharis is a towering love warrior and freedom fighter for precious poor people in the bowels of the American empire. This rich collection of essays is a powerful cacophony of prophetic voices that prefigure our beloved community."

—Cornel West, Dietrich Bonhoeffer Chair, Union
Theological Seminary, New York City

"Put down what you are doing and read this book now. It is clear eyes on Holy Scripture, an electric cord between heaven and earth, a bridge between what Muslims call *deen* and *dunya*: the cosmic world and the material world. *We Cry Justice* will bring you to your knees in prayer, it will connect you more deeply with your neighbor, and it will inspire you to organize for the world that God calls us to create."

—Eboo Patel, founder and president, Interfaith Youth Core

"What's just as important as reading the Bible is who we read it *with*. Our experiences and social location affect what we hear, and what we don't hear, as we read God's Word. As we read it together, we are reminded that the gospel is 'good news to the poor'—if it's not good news to the poor, then it is not the gospel of Jesus."

—Shane Claiborne, author, activist, co-founder of Red Letter Christians

"If you are inspired by the Poor People's Campaign, *We Cry Justice* is a must-read. It will inspire spiritual practice, scriptural reflection, and social action to transform your life—and the world."

—Valarie Kaur, Sikh American civil rights leader, author of
See No Stranger: A Memoir & Manifesto of Revolutionary Love

"*We Cry Justice* is good news! Read cover to cover or dip into random chapters; each chapter is an encounter with people living the Scripture with vibrant truth. This clarion call is the encounter that is needed to agitate and heal our nation and our planet."

—Sister Simone Campbell, SSS, lawyer, advocate,
and former executive director of NETWORK

"In these pages, an impressive group of contributors reminds us that we cannot talk about the love of God without taking seriously the need for justice for all God's children, especially the poor, the vulnerable, and the voiceless."

—The Most Rev. Michael B. Curry, presiding bishop
of The Episcopal Church and author of *Love Is the
Way: Holding on to Hope in Troubling Times*

"The book is an invitation to reflect in fresh ways on the urgency of faith and on the demanding crisis we face concerning issues of justice. This book is not to be 'scanned.' It is to be lived with while the justice-working, world-transforming Spirit of God does its relentless, indefatigable work."

—Walter Brueggemann, Columbia Theological Seminary

"Whether used as a personal devotional or as the foundation for communal discernment, *We Cry Justice* is an immediate must-have for anyone who takes seriously the biblical call to work for a just and abundant life for all of creation."

—Rev. Bruce Reyes-Chow, pastor, First Presbyterian Church of Palo
Alto, and former moderator of the Presbyterian Church (USA)

"The writers of *We Cry Justice* bring alive the meaning and the challenge of 'God's preferential option for the poor' for our world today. The message is clear: Doing justice is not an option for people of faith; rather, it is the work of God."

—The Very Reverend Kelly Brown Douglas, PhD, dean,
Episcopal Divinity School at Union, Bill and Judith Moyers
Chair in Theology, Union Theological Seminary

WE CRY JUSTICE

Reading the Bible with the
Poor People's Campaign

Edited by Liz Theoharis

Broadleaf Books
Minneapolis

CONTENTS

PART IV LEARN AS WE LEAD

FOREWORD

When I was growing up, sometimes the preacher was so clearly preaching truth from the Bible and challenging the ways of sin and injustice that somebody would say, "Cry loud, reverend. Cry loud!" In *We Cry Justice: Reading the Bible with the Poor People's Campaign*, Rev. Dr. Liz Theoharis and the other writers whose work is included in these pages know how to cry for justice. In a skillful and insightful way they instruct us, through the biblical witness, how to cry. They recognize that crying loud—crying out against injustice—is, according to the Bible, nonnegotiable.

This powerful book truly took me down memory lane. My grounding as a child was in a family of church leaders and social activists who saw no separation between the two. My father and mother were both active participants in the civil rights transformation and in the church, so when I consider what it means to read the Bible, my mind travels back to many of the things I heard expressed during my upbringing in the faith.

I'm the son of a pastor who was a "general evangelist" of our denomination; in other words, my father was often sent to build new congregations. Many times this began with a few people gathering for a Bible study. My mother was and is a church musician. She's a skilled hymnologist. When I accompanied her to choir rehearsal, I saw that she not only taught the hymns but also showed people that every hymn had a scriptural reference that undergirded the theological foundation. My mother taught more than the notes and the words in her rehearsals. She taught the Bible.

I come from a tradition in which vacation Bible school was non-negotiable in the summer. Sunday school was as important as morning worship, and memorization of Scripture was an important discipline in our spiritual development. In the homes of many of my relatives, eating dinner—especially on Sunday—was always preceded by individuals quoting Scripture. Despite the alluring aroma that kept pulling at every one of your tastebuds, you could not partake of the meal until everyone had quoted a verse. So the Bible was central to my development in the faith. In fact, we used to sing a song: "The B-I-B-L-E. Yes, that's the book for me. I stand alone on the word of God, the B-I-B-L-E" in many spaces.

But the Bible was not just a book of the church or a guide for personal devotion. It was the book of the movement. When we stood against social injustice, our stance had to be rooted in the word of God, the B-I-B-L-E. Early on, my father made sure I knew there was no separation between Jesus and justice. This was not a matter of mere political ideology but a central claim of our faith according to the authority of the bible—the B-I-B-L-E. I was taught that the Bible was the one book especially kept from the enslaved person and deliberately misinterpreted by the slave master. And so we were encouraged and pushed to read it.

We lived in one of the poorest regions of North Carolina. My parents challenged racism and economic injustice not just because they were unjust social realities but also because the Spirit requires a quarrel with the world's injustices. They found this mandate in the pages of the B-I-B-L-E. I was taught Micah 6: What doth the Lord require, but to do justice? Isaiah 58: We are called to be repairers of the breach, to loose the bands of wickedness. Luke 4: The spirit of the Lord is upon me to preach good news to the poor. Matthew 25: Inasmuch as you do to the least of these, you do it unto me. These were not just texts for memorization. They were the anchors around which an authentic Christian life must be centered.

All of this happened long before I went to seminary and read the great sermons of Dr. Martin Luther King Jr. This was my foundation before someone determined that there are more than two thousand scripture passages that speak to how we are called to treat the poor, the stranger, and those on the margins. Reading this book of devotions by Rev. Dr. Liz Theoharis and others takes me back to what I was taught about the centering position of the Bible for our communal and movement life together. I hope it also serves as a point of constant reflection for all those who will study its pages.

This movement called the Poor People's Campaign is not a movement for any one faith or any one religious tradition, but it is a movement in which the B-I-B-L-E has a place. Our *Sitz im Leben* gives us a particular hermeneutic and exegesis. The Bible gives us courage in the midst of struggle and an authoritative critique above the false and distorted authority of the systems of injustices that create poverty and inequality.

These reflections push us to reexamine, reimagine, and hear again the many great texts in the Bible that have something clear to say in our contemporary and continuing struggle for justice, truth, liberation, and love.

The title itself, *We Cry Justice*, grows out of a phrase often placed on the lips of the ancient prophets. The prophets were often described as crying: crying out, crying loud, crying on behalf of God. This cry had at least two dimensions. One is the cry of weeping and hurt because of the conditions of injustice, poverty, and pain perpetrated by forces of empire and deception. Sometimes the prophets like Jeremiah would say, "Oh that my head were a fountain of tears that I might cry on behalf of Israel." Jesus, in the Gospels, is described as crying over the city of Jerusalem because it has left undone the weightier matters of justice and faith, choosing to kill prophets rather than hear them. This sounds strangely similar to America today.

The other type of crying has the characteristic of a shout—a piercing yell that cuts through all of the noise of injustice and indifference. It is a blast like a trumpet, sounding an alarm. God tells the prophet Isaiah to cry loud and spare not and to tell the nation of her sins. This is the way Martin Luther King Jr., Fannie Lou Hamer, and many others then and now cry for justice. We have so many criers like this in the Poor People's Campaign.

For those of us in the faith, the Bible is not just a book. It is, as one hymn writer said, the "mighty word of God." As you read this book and reflect on its contents, we invite you to join us in the Poor People's Campaign as we cry for justice.

—Bishop William J. Barber II, DMin, president and senior lecturer of Repairers of the Breach and cochair of the Poor People's Campaign

INTRODUCTION

In a world broken by poverty, who does God call us to be and what does God call us to do? In the United States, where nearly half of the population is poor or low income, a dominant, distorted narrative blames the poor for their poverty. This narrative passes itself off as biblically rooted. But the good news of the poor proclaimed throughout the Bible rebukes political leaders and policies that degrade life, divide us from one another, and perpetuate the violence of poverty. Our sacred texts insist it is *poverty*, rather than the *poor*, that is immoral and sinful.

We Cry Justice demonstrates what it means to be devoted to the God of liberation, not a theology of empire nor of systems that degrade and destroy life. The chapters in this book are embodiments of lives and a movement devoted to building a world free from poverty, systemic racism, militarism, and ecological devastation. Through the reflections in this book—and, more importantly, through the leadership of the poor that has produced them—we express adoration to God and to God's commandments. We express our commitment to one another and dedication to building a movement to end injustice and to fight poverty, not the poor. Through sermons, protests, projects of survival, Bible studies, marches, songs, and more, we have devoted ourselves to God's work of liberation. These chapters are not just words on a page but are actions and expressions of our love for God, for one another, and for the world that God desires for all people.

The contributions in this book emerge from a movement seeking justice for all and rejecting the religion of empire. From Genesis to Revelation, our sacred texts teach us that poverty and injustice are not the will of God and that it is the responsibility of all those who claim to honor and worship God to work to end systemic racism, poverty, and all forms of injustice.

The contributors to this book read and write from the perspective of those who have been bruised and battered by empire. We have come forward to help establish God's "empire" (also called God's kingdom, *basileia*, reign) on earth as it is in heaven. After all, the founding story of the Bible is the exodus of people out of bondage, and the name God claims and proclaims is "I am the Lord your God, who brought you out of Egypt" (Exodus 20:2). The prophets remind those in power that God sides with the poor and judges those who "add house to house and join field to field" (Isaiah 5:8). The Gospels announce liberty to the captives, forgiveness of debts, a year of God's jubilee favor. Even Paul's Epistles center on building up mutual solidarity among the poor. In the biblical arc of justice, we are challenged to be chaplains for a movement rather than priests of empire.

The purpose of *We Cry Justice* is to provide strength, hope, and power for the more than 140 million poor and dispossessed people living in poverty in the midst of abundance, as well as to provide inspiration and guidance for those who stand with them. These devotionals are written by people in the struggle, many of whom are one storm, fire, health care crisis, or job loss away from deep poverty. In the words of Nic Smith, a fast-food worker and Fight for $15 activist, reminding us of the preacher, activist and theologian, Howard Thurman: "Our backs are against the wall and all we can do is push." Our hope is that these chapters will provide the spiritual nourishment to hold you through difficult days and the strength to sustain you in the movement to change the systems of injustice that have made us poor.

The prayers, quotations, reflections, and passages offered in this book are by and for "the least of these"—which is most of us. We pray that you might find hope in our solidarity and our collective action. Our power as poor people depends on our ability to unite across difference, to believe in our capacity and call as moral leaders, and to speak to the nation out of shared moral and religious convictions. The chapters in *We Cry Justice*, which have grown out of the work of a movement, are useful for individual reading, collective prayer or Bible study, or political education or spiritual formation; they might inspire actions, posters, or speeches at protests, marches, rallies, or prayer vigils. These devotional offerings empower us for just these tasks.

These reflections are written by those organizing through the Poor People's Campaign: A National Call for Moral Revival and related grassroots movements. The Poor People's Campaign is a diverse direct-action movement organized in more than forty states, anchored by the Kairos Center for Religions, Rights and Social Justice at Union Theological Seminary and by Repairers of the Breach. Together we are addressing the interlocking injustices of systemic racism, poverty, ecological devastation, militarism and the war economy, and the distorted moral narrative of religious nationalism. We are building power among poor and low-income leaders. Led by poor and dispossessed moral leaders on the front lines of struggle, the Poor People's Campaign puts forward solutions for ending poverty and its interlocking injustices. Clergy and other people of faith, activists, and academics serve as leaders within the campaign as well; many of us are also poor and are organizing among the poor to end poverty.

As a movement, we live a rhythm of themes—seasons that organize our collective life and work. These themes have guided our direct actions, political education, leadership development, and general work of ending poverty. This rhythm is captured in the six parts of this book.

Part I: Jubilee. Characterized by biblical stories and historical and contemporary examples in which every need is supplied—such as the garden of Eden, manna in the wilderness, the practice of jubilee, and life in the early Christian communities—this theme describes the antipoverty programs that run throughout the Bible. The season of Jubilee parallels Pentecost, when God's spirit was poured out onto a multiracial fusion movement of Jesus followers, as well as the season just after Pentecost, often known as Ordinary Time. These biblical narratives do not just provide our moral justification that everybody has a right to live; they show us how that reality can be achieved, in actions that ought to be ordinary in our lives and world.

Part II: Struggle and Lament. The Bible lifts up expressions of longing, mourning, and even anger at the way things are. More than seven hundred lives are cut short every day in the United States due to poverty. Millions of people in the United States die each year from inadequate health care. Crises in the form of pandemics, state-sanctioned violence, storms, and other disasters disproportionately affect the poor and people of color. In the richest country in human history, 140 million people are poor or just one emergency away from economic ruin. These are our people, our leaders, and our families, and we must mourn and wail and cry out to God for justice. The season of Struggle and Lament parallels the season of Lent in many Christian traditions; it is also a season in which the poor and dispossessed lament our struggles and call for the repentance of those who pursue policies and systems that are killing us.

Part III: The Days of Liberation. The story of Jesus's death and resurrection is the story of the state execution of an insurrectionist that ends in the triumph of God over the powers of death and destruction. This story of resurrection recalls the history of the Israelite people in the exodus and other passages of liberation and salvation. In this season, the Days of Liberation, we celebrate the many examples in which the liberation of the oppressed has triumphed over forces of evil. This time celebrates the many ways that the poor today and throughout history have been victorious over the forces of oppression and injustice.

Part IV: Learn as We Lead. Integral to the organizing and social change work of this movement is an understanding of praxis and leadership. As leaders of poor people's organizations, we learn through leading and lead through learning, knowing that our actions in movements for justice teach, draw from, and develop other leaders. Jesus led in much the same way. He was the leader of a poor people's movement, and in his work he linked teaching, leadership, and action. The liturgical season of Learn as We Lead acknowledges the necessity of education and leadership in building movements of the poor and dispossessed—throughout Scripture, throughout history, and in our work today. The biblical passages and devotional reflections offered in this liturgical season exemplify the organizing work of educating as we organize, talking as we walk.

Part V: The Advent of Revolution. Social movements and revolutions are built in stages. We see this throughout the Israelites' struggle for liberation and in the life and ministry of Jesus, as he built a movement of the poor against the empire of Rome. Texts that exemplify the stages of building a social movement characterize this season: the Advent of Revolution. They include the calls of the prophets, both biblical and contemporary, who demand a radical revolution of values and prepare the way for transformation from the bottom up.

Part VI: The Birth of a Movement. There are moments in every movement that mark the start of a new creation, a new process, a new organization, a birth of something new. In this season, we celebrate those moments in our collective histories, those moments in which we see clearly a rebirth toward liberation taking shape. In these times we retell, again and again, the freedom stories: how the emergence of a moral movement unites people across difference, from the history of the Israelite people and the Jesus movement to our work today. This season connects with the season of Epiphany in many Christian traditions and the baptizing of leaders, welcoming them and the spirit of justice into the movement.

The fifty-three chapters in this book can be used by individuals, families, congregations, and organizations. Individuals or families might use them as a weekly guide to reading Scripture, reflecting, praying, and taking action around the particular theme of each devotional entry. Organizations and congregations may collectively study the biblical text in relationship to the principles and work of the Poor People's Campaign. They can serve as inspiration for sermons, Bible studies, or protest speeches.

Each chapter includes an opening quotation, a Bible verse or passage, a devotional reflection on that passage's meaning for the poor and dispossessed today, and prompts at the end for further reflection, reading, and prayer. Individuals or groups can focus on one entry each week over the course of a year. A suggested guide is outlined below; there are, however, many more possibilities for using the chapters. Groups and individuals should use what best fits their context. Please share the wisdom you find with others in the Poor People's Campaign and the larger movement to end poverty and racism.

Suggested Weekly Reading Structure

Each day: Pray the prayer offered at the end of the entry.

Sunday: Read and reflect on the passage of Scripture for the week.

Monday: Read and reflect on the opening quotation. Find information about the leader and/or organization featured in the quotation to learn more.

Tuesday: Read the devotional reflection in the main body of the chapter.

Wednesday: Use the reflection questions to guide a solitary time of journaling or a group discussion.

Thursday: Read the additional suggested Scripture readings and reflect on their relationship to the entry of the week.

Friday: Read the contributor bio of the author of this week's reflection in the back of the book. Find information about the organizations and movements they are involved in. Pray for the author and the work of their organization.

Saturday: Consider what action you might take that is prompted by this week's reading and reflection. Perhaps it's something to implement in your life or with your congregation or organization. Or perhaps it's supporting the author's organization with an offering, through prayer, with an encouraging message, or by participating in an action.

We hope this book offers strength as you face the trials that systems of poverty, systemic racism, ecological devastation, and militarism have created. We pray these reflections, readings, and prayers inspire you to devote yourself, again and again, to building a better world for all—a world in which everyone is in and no one is out, just as God intended it.

We pray that an understanding of the Bible as a basis of liberation might guide you. We call for a Christian faith that leads not to a distorted moral narrative upholding death-dealing systems but to a truly abundant life. We invite you to become clear, committed, connected, and competent for the work of ending poverty and building a just world for all of God's children. We cry justice! Amen.

PART I
JUBILEE

1

IS ENDING POVERTY POSSIBLE?

Liz Theoharis

You Only Get What You're Organized to Take.

—SLOGAN OF THE NATIONAL UNION OF THE HOMELESS

READ: MATTHEW 26:1-16

"The poor you will always have with you" is what Jim Wallis of *Sojourners* calls the most famous Bible verse on poverty. Matthew 26:11 takes place in the context of a meal with Jesus's disciples, during which a woman comes and pours an alabaster jar of ointment on his head. This anointing scene happens in the town of Bethany, whose name means "House of the Poor" in Hebrew. It occurs directly after Jesus has turned over the tables and challenged the religious and political authorities for impoverishing people, and right before Judas betrays Jesus by turning him over, for thirty pieces of silver, to be crucified.

With this action, the woman anoints Jesus. He becomes *Christ*—the Greek word for "the anointed one"—in this scene. He is deemed Messiah: a ruler or prophet set apart by God to usher in a reign of justice. She prepares him for his burial. But the disciples don't understand the significance of this anointing, nor of Jesus's impending execution at the hands of the state.

The disciples criticize the woman for wasting (*apoleia*, the Greek word for "destroying") the ointment. Instead of breaking the jar and using it all, they say, the nard could have been sold for a year's salary and the money given to the poor. This idea—of earning lots of money and giving the proceeds to the poor—encapsulates how we often try to address poverty. Many Christians do charity work by buying and selling and then donating to the poor, but they never question how poverty was created in the first place.

When Jesus says, "The poor you will always have with you," he is quoting Deuteronomy 15, which says that there will be no poor person among you if you follow God's commandments. Those commands include forgiving debts, releasing the enslaved, paying people fairly, and lending money even when you won't get paid back. Deuteronomy 15:11, then, is essential. This verse claims that *because* people will not follow God's commandments, the poor will never cease to be in the land.

Nowhere in this passage, nor in the entire Bible, does God condone poverty. Jesus is reminding us that God hates poverty and has commanded us to end it by forgiving debts, raising wages, outlawing slavery, and restructuring society around the needs of the poor and pointed out Jesus and the prophets teachings on justice rather than bandaids. He is reminding the disciples that charity will not end poverty but instead will keep it with us always. Jesus is reminding his followers that he will be killed for bringing God's reign here on earth and that it is their responsibility to continue the quest for justice.

And, truly, poor people are continuing that quest. In June 2019, during a hearing of the budget committee of the House of Representatives, leaders of the Poor People's Campaign came to present what we've called the Poor People's Moral Budget. It's a study showing that the United States *does* have the money to end poverty, hunger, homelessness, and more; it's just that we do not have the political will to do so.

The walls of that House committee room rang with empty words that twisted what the Bible says about the poor. One representative remarked that he had never found any place in the Bible "where Jesus tells Caesar to care for the poor." Another suggested that Christian charity, not government-sponsored programs, is the key to alleviating poverty.

In response, members of our racially and geographically diverse group pointed out how interesting it was that the first representative—a self-proclaimed follower of Jesus—identified himself with Caesar. We detailed many of the passages of Scripture that urge us to organize society around the needs of the poor.

We did not end poverty in America that day. But one of our leaders, Aaron Scott, noted the power of what really happened. "We staged a full-on narrative takeover," Scott commented. "What I saw made it very clear that we have what it takes to force this government to atone for its sins" and really address poverty.

— REFLECT —

What message do you hear about poverty from faith leaders and government authorities? What are the people of God called to do in the face of poverty from this passage? How are people responding to poverty today? What issues are of particular concern to you?

— READ —

Deuteronomy 15:1-4. This is the passage Jesus cites when he is anointed as Christ in this story. This Scripture speaks to us about the role of laws and policies, rather than solely individual actions, in eradicating poverty.

— PRAY —

God of justice and life, we lift up to you 140 million of your people who are being abandoned in the midst of abundance. Grant us the wisdom, courage, and love to do your will: to organize society around the needs of the poor. May we strive to make earth as it is in heaven. Amen.

2

WHAT WE WISH FOR

Solita Alexander Riley

I wish I could live
Like I'm longin' to live

—BILLY TAYLOR, "I WISH I KNEW HOW IT WOULD FEEL TO BE FREE"

READ: DEUTERONOMY 15, 2 CORINTHIANS 6

We all carry so many wishes in our hearts. Some we utter aloud, and other wishes live on silently within us. One of my wishes is that we could all live free, joyful, and full lives. Yet so many of us who are poor are on the brink of despair. One reason? Debt.

There is nothing like debt to undermine the strength of a society. Debt easily becomes insurmountable, impossible to pay off. People crushed under the burden of medical, educational, and other kinds of debt. How many are not whole as a result? How many are healed but not restored, better skilled but not secure?

Put simply, God's economy does not include debt and poverty. Instead, it introduces practices to prevent it. This is where Deuteronomy 15 and 2 Corinthians 6 suggest hope. These passages offer the impetus to break down what stands between us and true freedom. God has a different reality in mind and calls us to work toward a society in which full life is possible.

Of the many laws set out in Deuteronomy, I wish we would take seriously the law described in chapter 15: the ritual practice of debt cancellation. In such times, an individual worked off what they owed to someone through enslavement or was forced into jail. Under these conditions, people could not fully participate in society. For this reason, in many societies of the ancient Near East, debts were canceled when a new leader took office so that the leader's reign would not face challenge and insurrection from a populace under duress. This also secured the health of the society by ensuring that all could fully participate in society.

Debt was deadly then, and it still is. How I wish debt cancellation were the law in our land! At the very least, we could apply the spirit of that law. As we see in Deuteronomy 15, there is first the call for individual practices that make sure all needs are met. These verses instruct people to freely lend to those in need so there will be no poor among them.

Charity and generosity have their place, but when people don't practice perfect charity and generosity, structural redress is necessary. So Deuteronomy 15 calls for structural practices as well. There need to be laws ensuring that people don't fall into deeper and deeper debt. Deuteronomy's plan makes a routine by which everyone is restored as debts are canceled.

Oh, how I wish we would be less confused about God's economy. Somehow we end up with laws that attach Work requirement to the need for food, clothing, housing, and medical care for yourself and your children. You don't have what you need because you are lazy, the false narrative tells us. Structurally, our society has chosen the absurdity of poverty and the deadliness of debt. Thankfully, projects of survival—such as yesterday's Black Panther health care clinics, today's food programs, and other operations—stand in to circulate resources. Still, more is needed.

Many of us wish for laws that guarantee jobs with living wages. We wish existing laws about affordable housing worked. We wish for health care for all. We wish to see the end of the school-to-prison pipeline and to see fully funded, equitable education instead. We wish for a tax structure that would make the wealthy and big businesses contribute their fair share of resources. We wish for money to come out of the military budget, out from our militarized police forces, and into our communities. We wish to live! All these wishes can become reality as we demand them.

We are told in 2 Corinthians 6 that now is the time. It is time to partner with God and with each other to create the world as God intends. It will not be easy, Paul tells us. We will endure much: riots, imprisonments, sleepless nights, hunger. If you are engaged in struggle, undoubtedly you have experienced some of these things.

You may be characterized as poor, but you are incredibly powerful, because what you are doing is building God's kingdom on earth! You are working with others and God to realize God's economy and to establish the principles of heaven right here and now.

— REFLECT —

You are powerful. What thoughts and feelings come up when you hear that truth? In what powerful ways are you addressing needs in your community? Are the laws and policies doing the same? How is God calling you to demand a fuller life for yourself and others?

— READ —

Acts 2:42–47. The early Jesus community reminds us of the power of coming together to support the needs of our community.

— PRAY —

Loving God, thank you for setting forward a principle by which all needs are met. You suggest laws to create an economy in which everyone thrives. Tend to us when we encounter structural harm and policy violence. Help us lift our voices, our arms, and our feet to create and demand the structures we all wish for. Amen.

3

JESUS WAS A POOR MAN

Jessica C. Williams

Don't laugh, folks: Jesus was a poor man.

—PHRASE WRITTEN ON A CANVAS COVERING ON THE MULE
TRAIN OF THE 1968 POOR PEOPLE'S CAMPAIGN

READ: MATTHEW 25:31-46

Jesus's last teaching to his disciples in the book of Matthew, often known as the parable of the last judgment or the story of the sheep and goats, is quoted by countless ministries that offer charity to "the least of these." Many say that it means we need to help those who are without food, shelter, and clothing.

But what if we take seriously the proclamation of the Mule Train organizers—that "Jesus was a poor man"? Does that change how we understand the passage about the sheep and the goats?

In the time and place in which Jesus ministered, most people lived under the subjugation of the Roman Empire and were considered expendable. Elite rulers extracted wealth from all the lands they conquered, pushing people to hunger, homelessness, and the brink of starvation—and sometimes over the edge into slavery and death. The Bible tells us that Jesus had no place to lay his head (Luke 9:58), which is another way to say he was homeless. Jesus was trained in carpentry—a form of manual labor akin to low-wage work today—and he relied on the hospitality of friends, many of whom were also poor, to share meals and lodging with him. Jesus, the disciples, and those to whom they ministered were poor, subjected, and oppressed. They were the expendables.

When the wagon riders in the Mule Train said "Jesus was a poor man," they were right. As part of the Poor People's Campaign in 1968, they carried that message from Marks, Mississippi, across the South, and up to Washington, DC, where they joined a six-week encampment on the National Mall called Resurrection City. The Mule Train's wagons were covered in canvas, on which the travelers wrote phrases to explain their mission: bringing attention to poverty in the United States and demanding systemic changes. They sought, as Rev. Dr. Martin Luther King Jr. said, "to lift the load of poverty."

"Jesus was a poor man" is a theological statement. It is more than saying "Jesus *cares about* the poor,"—how Matthew 25:31–46 is often interpreted. In Matthew 25, what is usually translated as "the least of these" is the Greek word *elachistoi*, which literally means "the smallest or most insignificant ones": in other words, the expendables. Jesus's identity as one of the least of these is not a romantic, charitable notion; it is Jesus's reality. He is saying that the social class of expendables are his people. The homeless, the poor, the incarcerated are Jesus's friends, family, disciples, and followers, and Jesus himself.

Matthew 25 is not a passage about charity. It's about structuring society around providing for the needs of all people, and it's about the leadership of the poor to create such change. In the stories of Jesus, the Mule Train organizers saw a shared experience. Along with Jesus, one of the poor and homeless in his time, they were joining the radical claim to agency and leadership of a movement for justice.

There is power in the proclamation that "Jesus was a poor man." I quilted this very phrase into the clergy stoles the cochairs of the Poor People's Campaign wear around their necks. On multiple occasions, authorities have told them that the statement on their stoles is "too political." They have had their stoles confiscated at protests.

In the United States, nearly half of us are poor and low income. The lack of governmental response to our basic human rights of living wages, housing, and health care is immoral. Whenever crisis hits, it is revealed even more clearly that "the least of these" are most of us. Understanding Jesus as a poor man affirms the agency of the poor as moral leaders in the movement to end poverty.

Interpretations of Matthew 25:31–46 that diminish Jesus's ministry to that of charity miss the gospel message and actually help to maintain inequality. But when we understand that the Roman Empire considered Jesus to be expendable—much the same way the United States considers poor and low-income people, nearly half of the population, to be expendable—we see that being a follower of Jesus means something deeper than charity. Being Christlike means joining a movement, led by the poor and dispossessed, to lift the load of poverty.

— REFLECT —

How might the understanding of Jesus as a poor man change how you understand his life, teachings, and ministry? How do you understand resurrection or salvation in light of this understanding of who Jesus is?

— READ —

Luke 2. This story of the birth of Jesus helps us explore how the Bible tells us that Jesus and his family were poor.

— PRAY —

Holy God, you sent your Son into the world not to condemn it but to change it. Strengthen the leaders from poor communities whom you have called into the ministry of building a social movement. Amen.

4

GOD CREATED ENOUGH

Daniel Jones

> The whole of the Bible . . . has the arc of justice. This arc starts with the exodus and manna, which is most likely a response to Joseph and Pharaoh setting up a system where a few religious and political leaders amassed great wealth at the expense of the people. . . . It runs through Deuteronomy and the legal codes, which describe how society and our political and religious leaders are supposed to release slaves, forgive debts, pay people what they deserve, and distribute funds to the needy. It then continues through the prophets who insist that the way to love and honor God is to promote programs that uplift the poor and marginalized, and who decry those with religious and political power who cloak oppression in religious terms and heretical theology.
>
> **—LIZ THEOHARIS**

READ: EXODUS 16:15-25

As soon as the Israelites finish singing and celebrating their liberation from slavery, they find themselves thirsty, hungry, and full of doubts.

They've left the empire of Pharaoh behind, but they haven't yet found a new way to organize their life together. Unclear whether and how to move forward, they cry out to God to meet their material needs. Exodus 16:15–25 describes God's answer to this cry, a response that shows us God always creates enough for everyone's needs. The response also reveals what God intends for our life together, distilling the principles we must use to organize our society—principles that point us in a very different direction from our present course.

At the beginning of 2020, just ten companies were sitting on a combined hoard of $350 billion in cash. From 2010 to 2019, the five hundred largest public companies in the United States spent more than $9 trillion—the vast majority of their profits—paying their shareholders and pumping up the price of their stocks. This immense wealth is a reflection of the great abundance in our world today. It's the wealth that God has put on this planet and that is created by the combined and collective labor of billions of people. Drawn into the hands and pockets of a tiny minority, however, it piles up in great heaps, spent on speculation or hidden away in tax havens while millions are hungry, homeless, sick, poisoned, and locked up.

This is not what God desires from us. Nor is this what God wants for us.

When the Israelites cry out in hunger, God sends them food, the manna. God instructs them: "Everyone is to gather as much as they need." So they do. Moses also warns them not to take more than they need and not to hoard any of the manna overnight. But the Israelites ignore God. By morning, the hoarded food is rotten, infested with maggots, and of no use to anyone.

This is, in fact, the very first concrete commandment that God gives to the newly freed Israelites: to gather only what they need and to use what they gather. This basic idea is present throughout the Torah, and the prophets take it up again and again: God provides enough for all of us, and God has commanded us to share it with each other and not gather it jealously and fearfully for ourselves. This living abundance goes to rot when it is stored up for its own sake and kept from serving the needs of God's children. When food, land, labor, or debts are held, accumulated, and controlled by too few for too long, poverty grows, society fractures, and crisis looms. What the powerful thought was their strength eventually turns into their ruin.

God condemns the private accumulation of wealth because it's inseparable from the general impoverishment of society. Instead, we're called to reorganize our lives together. We're called to make a final break from the faithless lie of scarcity and embrace the fullness of our abundant world. And this call is all around us. It's in the demands to stop rationing health care and to stop closing hospitals in cities, small towns, and rural areas. It's in the mobilizations to prevent evictions and move families into empty homes. It's in the demand for food stamps, living wages, and guaranteed income.

All of these voices and struggles carry a fundamental message from God: There is enough here. Share it. Take only what you need, and care for one another.

— REFLECT —

What message does this passage carry about the causes of poverty? What does it say to us about the principles that should organize our collective life?

— READ —

Isaiah 1:31. This verse helps us perceive the deadly judgment and ultimate ruin brought to societies marked by oppression and those who cause it.

— PRAY —

Living Breath of the World, every day you bless us with the abundance of your creation. Give us strength to break the bonds that keep billions hungry, homeless, overworked, underpaid, and oppressed. Come near to us, put our enemies to flight, and allow us to restore the wholeness of your teaching. Amen.

5

GIVE US THIS DAY OUR DAILY BREAD

Melanie Mullen

> To those who have hunger, give bread; and to those who have bread, give the hunger for justice.
>
> —BENEDICTINE PRAYER

READ: MATTHEW 6:9-13

Many of us learn the words of the Lord's Prayer as children. We say them throughout life: in times of joy and sorrow, at weddings and at funerals, on dressed-up Sunday mornings and in pajamas at night. With these words we ask for rescue in times of crisis, and we pray for well-being and safety—the daily bread of survival.

Jesus teaches the Lord's Prayer as part of the larger Sermon on the Mount. In that sermon he offers radical, spiritual survival strategies for the poor, the powerless, and other outsiders of the empire. He helps them understand how and why they matter to God, and he talks to God in a radically new way.

When Jesus prays to "Our Father" in his hillside talk, he opens up the heart of inclusion. Suddenly his impromptu classroom includes anyone passing by, not just the individual disciples at his feet, so that they can listen to his liberating and life-giving words. For the first time, an entire community is invited to think of themselves as members of God's family.

They are emboldened to pray not only for their individual souls but for the collective well-being of the entire society—for other children of God and their siblings in Christ.

For Jesus's disciples, the prayer redefined their status according to the relationship formed by being children of "Our Father." Being able to lift up their needs to the Creator we all have in common helped them to remember who and whose they are.

These words still invite those of us hungry for justice to pray to our common God and to claim our daily bread. We are all children of one Creator, and we all get to derive legitimacy as humans with equal dignity. Ultimately, regardless of our social, legal, or economic status, this prayer draws us together and equalizes us as children of God.

The Lord's Prayer speaks to the anxiety of those wondering how to make rent or put food on the table. Too many people have to pray for daily bread because of severe and sudden economic downturns, pandemics, or the long-standing insecurity of lost jobs and low wages. But the Lord's Prayer also helps us remember that we are under the care of a God who rained down manna in the exodus. Cries of hunger and fear grieve God, especially when those cries result from greed, hoarding, and economic exploitation.

The prayer for our daily bread powers some of the most urgent cries for justice. When the COVID-19 pandemic broke out, conditions were particularly dangerous in places like California's Yuba County Jail and the Mesa Verde Immigration and Customs Enforcement (ICE) detention facilities. As the number infected with the virus rose in those facilities, detainees gave up physical bread during a hunger strike. They took up a protest when imprisonment became virtually a death sentence. Their petitions for safety and human dignity were matched in area Lutheran churches, and soon the whole local community was amplifying their prayers with a national vigil. Praying the Lord's Prayer together gave them the spirit and sustenance to petition against injustice. It strengthened them as they exposed the state-sponsored brutality and reprehensible conditions in ICE detention facilities.

California's immigrant hunger strikers and their allies drew sustenance from the Lord's Prayer. Its proclamations offered them daily assurance of God's vision for a justice-filled world. The Lord's Prayer sustained their activism and made them bold enough to proclaim that those who have enough must demand daily bread for those who don't.

These prayer lessons, passed down to us from Jesus and the first disciples, show us how to continually ask for the support of God to transform oppression into liberation. They remind us that we are united in equality as God's children, and they point us toward a different kind of community. This is not just the community as the world is now but the one in which bread is shared, those who are homeless and poor are housed, those who have been divided are reconciled, and captives are freed.

— REFLECT —

As children of God, hungry for justice, we know that daily bread can take on many forms. What is the daily bread you and your community need to survive right now? How can we act to ensure those around us are given their daily bread—individually, communally, and systemically?

— READ —

Luke 1:46-55. Mary praises God, who lifts the lowly, humbles mighty rulers, fills the hungry, and empties the rich.

— PRAY —

"Loving God, the hallowing of your name echo through the universe! The way of your justice be followed by the peoples of the world!.... With the bread we need for today, feed us.... Now and forever." (From *A New Zealand Prayer Book (He Karakia Mihinare o Aotearoa)*)

6

OF THE POOR, FOR THE POOR

Colleen Wessel-McCoy

Organizations like ours could not continue to depend on grants and other resources from foundations at a time when everyone is caught in the economic squeeze and governmental repression that exists in this nation today. The types of organizing the action campaigns that NWRO [the National Welfare Rights Organization] continues to wage against the nation's oppressive institutions almost requires us to be self-sufficient, because too many of those foundations and funding groups are running scared-too scared to deal with us.

—JOHNNIE TILLMON

READ: 2 CORINTHIANS 8:1-7, 13-15

Paul often writes about poor people sharing what little they have with other poor people. "The collection," as this fund has often been called, was money raised by Jesus communities throughout the Roman Empire and sent to the poor leaders of the new Jesus movement based in Jerusalem—who Paul calls "the Lord's people." Paul writes about this collection for the poor in almost all of his major letters, so we know it is very important to him.

The Roman Empire wanted the nations it had conquered to be divided against one another and united only in their obedience to Caesar. If the empire could keep them separate, it could keep them in check. Money was collected and sent to Caesar and his elites—more money than people could afford to send—and the people were left starving.

The collection Paul talks about, however, is quite the opposite. It is a way for the poor to build a movement that brings together all the nations under God's laws of equality and all having what they need. It is not about taxes, tithes, or charity. It is not about a prosperity gospel promising to make people rich if they give away their last coin. Instead, it is a way to care for one another. It is a way to help one another survive under conditions of severe poverty. And it is a way to fund the building of a movement, in defiance of the ruling Roman Empire, where the kingdom of God is on earth as in heaven and all have their daily bread.

In 1966, the National Welfare Rights Organization (NWRO) came together out of local chapters of mothers who had helped each other navigate the welfare system. They'd share experiences with getting a welfare case reinstated or handling difficult social workers. As they grew in number, they were able to take on bigger and bigger campaigns and start to impact welfare policy for the whole country.

They made sure families were getting their full allotments for school clothes, winter coats, and furniture. They fought back against work requirements for moms, saying raising kids is work—and for moms who wanted to work, they fought for childcare. In some areas they got utility companies to drop deposits for poor families. They expanded food stamps and WIC (Women, Infants, and Children) benefits. They changed "man in the house" rules, under which social workers could come into your living space to look for evidence that you didn't live alone. By making fair hearings a right, they challenged racist biases, punitive caseworkers who hid behind complex rules, and arbitrary treatment. They were leaders in the 1968 Poor People's Campaign. And they rejected the scapegoating of poor women and asserted the right to housing, food, income, and raising their own children. They made big changes—and organized for even bigger changes—by starting with mutual support, helping each other get the welfare they were entitled to receive.

At its height, NWRO, led by Black women, was the largest organization of poor people in the United States, organizing poor moms across the dividing lines of race and ethnicity. Johnnie Tillmon, NWRO's first chair-person, developed an organizing model that did not rely on funders, who often call the shots on what work organizations do. Rather, in this model, the poor themselves could fund their organization. Because there were so many poor people, if every poor person on welfare in the nation would give just fifty cents, they would have a collective budget of millions of dollars. Even though they were poor, their unity was a force to be reckoned with.

Like the communities in Macedonia and Corinth and Jerusalem, the mothers of NWRO showed the genius of a collection *of* the poor and *for* the poor. Together, they demonstrated how the poor make a way out of no way.

— REFLECT —

When have your needs been met by someone who wasn't much better off than you? In 2 Corinthians, Paul refers several times to the Macedonians' and Corinthians' giving from poverty to other poor communities as "grace." How does that change your understanding of what grace is? How have you shared grace with others?

— READ —

Exodus 16. Equality is a central principle in God's kingdom. NWRO, Paul's 2 Corinthians letter, and this Exodus story all give us insight as to how equality is made manifest.

— PRAY —

God, your miracles surround us. Guide us in fulfilling your will that we may live together in equality, sharing your abundance. With overflowing joy, we give ourselves to you and to each other. We give out of our poverty to support each other as we organize together for justice. Give us such grace today and every day. Amen.

7

A HARVEST FOR ALL PEOPLE

Claire Chadwick

> The church must be reminded that it is not the master or the servant of the state, but rather the conscience of the state. It must be the guide and the critic of the state, and never its tool. If the church does not recapture its prophetic zeal, it will become an irrelevant social club without moral or spiritual authority.
>
> —MARTIN LUTHER KING JR.

READ: DEUTERONOMY 24

The laws contained in Deuteronomy 12–26 were written for the Israelites as a set of self-governing rules. How do we live together after years of slavery and oppression? How do we take care of ourselves, each other, and those who encounter our community? How do we avoid repeating the sins of empire, like idolatry and impoverishment and division?

This set of chapters, known as the Deuteronomic Code, is not simply a set of spiritual rules or even laws for how a religious community should act. The codes are rules for how a governmental system should be put into place.

In the particular passage of Deuteronomy 24, the reader learns that parts of the harvest should be kept aside in order to care for those who need it. The harvest is not just for those who reap it, for those who sow it, or for those who can afford it. The harvest is for *all* people: those living in the community and those who visit.

This is a shining example of what it is to care for one another. We provide everyone we encounter with what they need in order to live, and we do this in opposition to oppression. We provide for all so that no one is in need among us, because we know what it is like to be in need. The Israelites had known deep oppression and slavery in previous generations. They sought not to repeat the sins of the past. They wanted to keep themselves from eventually becoming the oppressors, so they organized themselves in such a way as to maintain compassion in their governmental system.

How can we read this commandment about community justice and not feel convicted by the flagrant injustices in our own communities? When we were first in the midst of the global pandemic, in an already inequitable society, our country and so many of our states and local communities decided that opening back up for the sake of the economy was more important than the lives of those who were being sacrificed.

As an "essential worker," I recognize that my life has been given up, time after time, as a sacrifice for the sake of economy, for the sake of business, for the sake of someone else's wealth. When my state issued a stay-at-home order, I continued to work in a big-box store so that others could get essential items. I contracted COVID-19 during this time, even while my employer had taken precautions to keep us safe. I struggled through a month of debilitating symptoms, gut-wrenching medical bills, and depressing isolation.

What does the Deuteronomic Code tell us about the sin of sacrificing people for the benefit of an economy that never served us to begin with? What does it say about the sins of our country when essential workers are only essential insofar as we can provide others the goods they desire?

Having recovered but still struggling with ongoing symptoms, I returned to work. I live in a state in which the governor traded political power for the well-being of residents. The state had opened back up, with very few restrictions, and soon the number of those infected with COVID-19 exploded. I was no longer one of the few at my job who had experienced the virus. My coworkers and I continued to work during a pandemic that the government chose to ignore. We continued to put our-selves and our families at risk.

As I write this, the number of those infected and dying continues to rise. Down the road, coming for us and other workers are medical bills that cannot be paid, jobs that will be lost because of sickness, and evic-tion notices. All this will happen while the billionaires of this country get richer.

And before religious extremists hijack and distort what the Bible has to say on this issue, let me return us to the Deuteronomic Code. We are charged with taking care of one another, with saving the grain for others in our community. How can we call ourselves a moral nation when we ignore such a charge?

— REFLECT —

In what ways has God called on us to care for one another? How is this reflected in the nation's economic system? Where has this nation fallen short? How do you and your household continue to experience God's care?

— READ —

Luke 12. This Scripture helps us see that we are each inherently worthy and cared for by God, with abundant provision that is meant for all.

— PRAY —

God of justice and compassion, hear our prayer. Bring us together so that we understand the plight and the insight of our sisters and brothers. Give us comfort as we bind our wounds and fire as we fight for justice. May we strive to truly follow your will and to always take care of one another. Amen.

8

THE POWER TO CRY JUSTICE

Idalin Luz Montes Bobé

> "[After] Jesus was lynched, [the disciples] were told to go to Jerusalem and wait until they got the power. . . . How did they get it? When they became of 'one accord'–when they were organized. It was when they were all agreed together that there was power. So Pentecost is unity–a condition met."
>
> **—CLAUDE WILLIAMS**

READ: ACTS 2:1-21

I was born and raised in the hood, and I have battled systemic poverty my entire life. As we live in times of sickness and hunger, poverty and violence, the fragility of our societies' structures is being fully exposed. Our government looks after corporations and leaves our people scrambling. Black bodies are being murdered by the state and by vigilantes. For some people, despair at all this injustice is new. For me, despair is all too familiar.

In Acts 2, the Holy Spirit comes to—and *into*—the disciples of Jesus. The Spirit enables the disciples to speak in such a way that others, no matter where they come from or what language they speak, can understand.

That same Spirit is at work today, and we can still feel the power and unity of that moment. That Spirit is the power that affirms for us the worthiness we are so often denied and reminds us that we are beloved. It gives us the power to cry justice in the face of oppression, and claim human rights as our inheritance, and grow our movement. When we cry out in protest, we hear, see, and feel the Spirit moving.

We read that when the Holy Spirit comes in this way to the disciples, they are mocked and called drunkards. We should remember that they are very vulnerable at this time. Their leader, Jesus, has just been executed by the state, and they are already at the bottom of the power structure in the Roman Empire. Yet they carry a life-affirming message, and through their unity, they are filled up with a spirit that sustains them. Peter steps forward to oppose the lies being told about this freedom movement. He reminds everyone there that the disciples are fulfilling what has been proclaimed: that in God's kingdom, young and old, men and women, and especially the poor will all prophesy.

To prophesy is to carry a message of the mind of God to a particular situation. God's mind is always on justice, on the end of oppression, on fully living. This empowerment, carrying God's unmistakable message, is exactly what happens when movements for liberation take root. The Holy Spirit shows up right there in all protests.

Many people living in the United States share my story, but they remain silent for fear of being shamed and called lazy. We know from experience that when we cry out—in any language we know—we'll be criticized, just like the disciples. We'll be called drunkards, criminals, and worse. Those in power will try to deny our message by attacking who we are and how we speak, and they will shift the blame for our problems back onto us. But when you protest and organize together, the Holy Spirit comes and affirms for you that you *do* matter, that you *are* worthy, and that you *must* cry out for justice. Despair and hopelessness no longer lie heavy on your spirit.

That sensation you feel at a protest? It must be similar to the feeling of Pentecost, where the Holy Spirit comes with a message for all to hear. We see the youth rising up, screaming that our lives matter, and these voices are not to be mocked. We are sharing our stories in different languages and phrases, but the meaning all comes down to one thing: we are oppressed people, and we are tired of living in a society that tells us profit matters more than our lives.

Our systems try to shame us, silence us, and divide us, but the Holy Spirit unites us and imparts the ability to deliver a message. We will not be divided, ridiculed, or vilified. We all have messages about defending life—messages that God wants others to hear. The Holy Spirit is moving in our midst.

— REFLECT —

What holy message is being delivered when people cry justice? Why do the media and others vilify the voices of people who stand in protest, showing only burning cars and buildings while hiding the message that's there in that burning? Where do you feel the Holy Spirit in your community?

— READ —

Matthew 5:1–12. In the Sermon on the Mount, Jesus melds peace and justice. Which do you fear more: facing persecution or standing up for justice?

— PRAY —

Dear Holy Spirit, thank you for reminding us that we are worthy and that human rights are our inheritance. Thank you for the power of protest, for a way to collectivize our voices and share lessons. Holy Spirit, fall upon us so we may speak and be heard, our systems may reflect God's thoughts, and justice and care will flow. Amen.

9

WHEN YOUR KIN FALL INTO DIFFICULTY

Tejai Beulah

> "In order for us as poor and oppressed people to become a part of a society that is meaningful, the system under which we exist has to be radically changed. . . . It means facing a system that does not lend itself to your needs and devising means by which you can change that system."
>
> —ELLA BAKER

READ: LEVITICUS 25:8-55

Leviticus 25:8–55 outlines God's ordination of the year of Jubilee. This year, which is to take place every fifty years, offers a model for how to equalize the nation's internal economy by offering relief and protections to the poor, families, and resident aliens. Accommodations are made to prohibit the enslavement of people in debt. Essentially, the Jubilee insists that the wealthy pay a fair share of taxes for the economic benefit of all in society, especially the poor.

Several times throughout this passage, the wealthy are instructed with the phrase "If any of your kin fall into difficulty" (25:35 NRSV). Following that phrase comes a list of duties to be performed on behalf of those in need. The wealthy–and wealth nations–are asked to follow these instructions as an act of trust and obedience to God and as a sign of unity of all God's people.

The Leviticus passage has significant implications for us today, especially for our understanding of US history. Our resources come from God, and so we have a duty to provide for all God's people. At the same time, this Scripture helps us to understand why poverty exists, and has existed, in the United States. To start, the United States does not insist that the wealthy pay a fair share of taxes to accommodate the needs of everyone in our society. Capitalism encourages the rich to get richer— and, inevitably, the poor become poorer.

Yet it is the poor who ultimately push this society to become as "meaningful" and transformative as Ella Baker believed it could be when she said the words above in 1969. Poor people, not the wealthy, are the ones who organize when their kin—that is, other human beings—fall into difficulty.

Ella Baker believed the poor and oppressed could change the system of the United States. She demonstrated this belief by organizing and training unemployed college students, many of whom made up the Student Nonviolent Coordinating Committee (SNCC), the premier student organization of the civil rights movement in the sixties. SNCC students were dispatched to the Mississippi Delta, a geographic region that was thoroughly segregated and ravaged by poverty. They befriended Delta sharecroppers, studied US law and politics with them, and encouraged them to register to vote.

Perhaps the greatest figure to emerge from the Mississippi movement was Fannie Lou Hamer, a middle-aged sharecropper who became a political activist. She radically challenged the white supremacist democratic establishment at the local, state, and national levels from 1962 to 1977. In addition to her political work, Hamer fought against malnutrition, compulsory sterilizations, inadequate education, and other barriers poor Black people in Mississippi faced. She persevered in her attempts to change the system even as her own health steadily declined. She died of cancer at the age of fifty-nine on March 14, 1977.

Decades later, poor and oppressed freedom fighters in the United States are still doing the work of changing the system through meaningful advocacy. Thousands of workers are organizing to demand fair wages, as evidenced in the Fight for $15 movement. The poor are leading the charge for fair access to health care, as Put People First! PA shows. Those threatened with eviction are organizing rent strikes. Across the country, people are protesting the killing of Black people by cops. And knowing the poor are the front lines of the environmental crisis, we are organizing for big policy changes to address environmental concerns.

Leviticus puts it simply: society as a whole should make provisions for the poor. US history shows that poor people make provisions for themselves and for one another. They know how to provide for the kin among us who struggle, against enormous odds. Perhaps the key to Jubilee in the United States is to look to the poor, not to the wealthy, for leadership.

— REFLECT —

What would Jubilee look like today? How can you influence the establishment of the Jubilee in your community?

— READ —

Matthew 25:31-40. The king in this passage has much to teach us about caring for people in need.

— PRAY —

God, help us to change the system. Help us to model teaching on Jubilee in the United States and around the world. Ashe and amen.

10

THE LAW THAT DISINHERITS IS NOT GOD'S LAW

Brigitte Kahl

> "Poor and homeless white, brown, and black families came together and set up a homeless encampment as part of a just and joint struggle to save our lives. There in unity we would periodically pray and sing hymns. One gospel song especially moved us all. It went, 'I need you, you need me. We're all a part of God's body. Stand with me, agree with me. We're all a part of God's body. It is God's will, that every need be supplied. You are important to me, I need you to survive.'"
>
> **—WILLIE BAPTIST**

READ: GALATIANS 3:26-4:7

A liberating passage, Galatians 3-4 presents us with some challenges. It discusses slavery, which, in the United States context and others, brings to mind the terrible system and legacy of owning people as chattel, as property. And although Roman slavery was different from US chattel slavery, it was an unjust system of some people buying, selling, and exploiting human beings nonetheless. If you can for a moment, hold your definition of slavery in suspension, and restage this text. Think of Paul telling the Jesus followers in Anatolia a story. Perhaps it is not just a story that happens in a distant land to a distant people who are confused about their identity, suffering under the rule of the Roman empire; perhaps it is a story for our world today. Here's how that scene may have played out.

There was a rich man. He held a large estate that was run by slaves, who did all the work in the fields and in the house. And the slaves were run by the managers, who were run by the master, who was the owner of all and a rich man.

There also was a child, who happened to be the heir of the estate. But the rich man had not the slightest interest in children and told the managers and overseers to take care of the boy until he would be ready to inherit. The managers did as they were told and put the kid into the slave quarters, where the managers had everything under control. And thus the son, who was the rich man's heir, grew up among slaves, separated from the one to whom he belonged and watched, even ruled over, by guards instead.

Now what happens, Paul asks the Anatolians, when the child is old enough and the father lets him step in as heir?

Well, somebody says, he will probably find it odd to have slaves now who serve him. But I bet after a while he'll like it, another one ponders; I bet he'll start to boss the slaves around like his father does. At this point someone else jumps in: You always think the worst our superiors. What if this boy becomes a decent master or boss—one who gives his slaves a nice gift for their birthday and maybe even a small monthly allowance so that they can put out some extra food for the kids?

Nobody notices that Paul is getting agitated. Is this all you can come up with? he finally explodes. Looking at their puzzled faces, he takes a deep breath and continues: You are telling the story as it is always told, in which the heir keeps the system of slavery in place. All you are debating is a slightly better or worse turn things might take, with superiors playing trump cards as they would normally. But this is the wrong story altogether; it's not God's story or the story of the faith. This story is not about what the heir does to the enslaved, but about who the enslaved actually are, who they always were. It's about the identity of the enslaved first and foremost, and about the work of the heir to reinforce their true identity as heirs of God.

Listen, Paul says: The heir in our story was "no different from a slave" (4:1), right? Remember, the heir is separated from his father, under the rule of the guards, working. In terms of the guards' treatment, the heir's relationship to the father seems to be of no consequence; indeed that relationship may as well not exist. So in this way, we can say the heir is enslaved. And, in God's story, this means: If the heir is a slave like every other slave, then *every* slave is an heir—not just this particular one, who happened to be born to the right father with the right slip of paper as his birth certificate. All of us! You and I and all who are under the thumb of the Roman masters, who make their fortune from our labor and our land: we're heirs too.

Read this: Jesus is crucified, executed by the Romans but still God's son. But when it turns out that he is God's son, he doesn't just move up to his father's mansion and leave the other slaves behind in the dungeon or otherwise suffering under the Romans. He shows up with them as his sisters and brothers—those who are legitimate children of the father like him. They *all* deserve their equal share in the inheritance.

Don't you think this will make the rich father, his notaries and lawyers cringe?

But in God's story, the father doesn't even mind! On the contrary: he likes to have children around being noisy. He even sends the shouting spirit of his son into our hearts to make us cry out in different languages, "Abba! Padre! Father!" For God wants God's children to claim not only the inheritance that is ours but also our birthright as human beings. Even if we don't have the right piece of paper with the right stamp on it—even if we are undocumented, poor, migrants, homeless—the law that has disinherited us is not God's law. We are *all* heirs, even if we have not inherited a single penny from our parents and own nothing to hand down to our children other than our debts.

This is what Paul is talking about in Galatians when he writes that there is no longer Jew or Greek, slave or free, male or female. All of us are one in Christ Jesus. None of us should be enslaved. All of us are children. All of us are heirs.

— REFLECT —

What is the story you tell about your identity? What do you say is your inheritance? How might God react to some of the things you're saying? In what ways do you repeat the dominant narrative? Who is crying out a new narrative about your true identity and inheritance, and how can you join in the storytelling?

— READ —

Exodus 16:13-21. In this Scripture, we encounter God's children while wandering in the bleakness; they are hungry, unprotected, uncertain. God provides for them and teaches them a new economy of sharing that leaves no one in need (and curbs the greed).

— PRAY —

God our father, give us strong faith. Give us a loud voice to cry out for everybody to hear that we are human beings, your children and heirs. Amen.

11

JESUS CAME TO SET IT OFF

Erica N. Williams

"I choose to identify with the underprivileged. I choose to identify with the poor. I choose to give my life for the hungry. I choose to give my life for those who have been left out of the sunlight of opportunity. I choose to live for and with those who find themselves seeing life as a long and desolate corridor with no exit sign. This is the way I'm going. If it means suffering a little bit, I'm going that way. If it means sacrificing, I'm going that way. If it means dying for them, I'm going that way, because I heard a voice saying, 'Do something for others.'"

—MARTIN LUTHER KING JR.

READ: LUKE 4

The phrase "set it off" means to start a fight, or to get into it. We see in Jesus's inaugural message in Luke 4:18–21 that he boldly declares he came to do just that.

In this passage, Jesus has a *sankofa* moment: a moment of going back to the past to retrieve what is useful for today. He reflects on his own lineage of freedom fighters when he declares he is here to get in on what

Isaiah prophesied! The passage in Luke 4:18–19 is referring to the prophecy in Isaiah 61:1–3, which foretells that a Messiah will come to restore the Israelites from the Babylonian captivity. Announcing the good news is a theme throughout Isaiah. The people have been promised that they will be set free, and Jesus wants his people to know that he has been sent to bring liberation to them and to all people.

Jesus was a brown-skinned Palestinian Jew who grew up in Nazareth, a town that was poor and marginalized, ruled and militarized by the Roman Empire. The society was dominated by oppression of the peasant class as well as by purity codes and patriarchal concepts. Peasant societies were marked by an enormous gulf between rural peasants and urban ruling elites. They were politically oppressive, economically exploitative, and religiously legitimated. The purity ideology central to the structure of these societies was created by the temple elites and generated a class of untouchables and outcasts. The patriarchal structure ensured that men held all of the power and that women were excluded.

Jesus, who was a peasant himself, saw all of these things happening to his people. He knew that he could not be a chaplain of the empire but was sent to be a prophet of God—one anointed by God and the people to do the work of love, justice, and liberation.

We see Jesus set it off in a nonviolent way during his ministry: he gives sight to Bartimaeus, and he stops a woman from being stoned to death for adultery by telling her accusers that anyone without sin could be the first to throw a stone (John 8:7). In Jesus's final week before being crucified (during the Passover, which celebrates the Jewish people's defeat of slavery), Jesus goes into the temple. There he sets it off by flipping the tables of the money changers and declaring that God's house is a place of prayer and not a den of thieves.

A man considered a nobody set it off by showing radical love and revolutionary compassion and by speaking truth to power. Jesus turned the world right side up. The empire thought it had shut Jesus down by lynching him, but all it did was plant a seed.

That seed has produced a great harvest of freedom fighters such as Harriet Tubman, Frederick Douglass, Fannie Lou Hamer, Ella Josephine Baker, Septima Clark, and Martin Luther King Jr. We must honor those who fought the good fight before us, but we must remember that the fight did not stop with them.

Each of us is being called to set it off. It does not matter what your pedigree is: God is calling you to stand for truth and justice. That is why

I have dedicated my life to ending poverty now. When you have over 140 million poor and low-income folks in the richest nation in the world, it is time to set it off.

So I plan to set it off in every space and place until every person has an adequate place to stay, food to eat, health care, and all the other basic things they deserve. I promise to give my all to the righteous struggle until I give my last breath. Will you join me?

— REFLECT —

Ask yourself: Would I be considered a priest of the empire or a prophet of God? What issues do I see in my community that are calling for someone—maybe even someone like me—to set it off?

— READ —

Revelation 21. In this passage, we glimpse the new reality made possible as we set it off.

— PRAY —

Creator, in your infinite mercy and grace, give us the strength and courage to be doers and not just hearers of your word. Let us be swift to stand against the empire and the injustices we see. Let us not continue in our complacency of playing it safe while the breath that you gave to your people is being deflated each day by poverty, racism, militarism, ecological devastation, and the distorted moral narrative of Christian nationalism. Grant us the spirit of the great liberator, Jesus Christ, who set into motion a new world. Ashe and amen.

PART II
STRUGGLE AND LAMENT

12

YOU MUST LET US WAIL

Stephen Pavey

"There are days–this is one of them–when you wonder what your role is in this country and what your future is in it. How, precisely, are you going to reconcile yourself to your situation here and how you are going to communicate to the vast, heedless, unthinking, cruel white majority that you are here. I'm terrified at the moral apathy, the death of the heart, which is happening in my country. These people have deluded themselves for so long that they really don't think I'm human. And I base this on their conduct, not on what they say. And this means that they have become in themselves moral monsters."

—JAMES BALDWIN

READ: AMOS 5

Amos was an eighth-century Hebrew prophet sent by God to warn a nation of its unjust and moral disordering. That nation was not that far from the United States today.

In Amos's time, the Northern Kingdom of Israel had extended its lands and increased its influence over trade routes, which brought great economic prosperity to the nation. God's vision of society—in which wealth is shared and the needs of every member of society are met—was fracturing because of rampant materialism, greed, corruption, and bribery. Like we see in the United States, the gap between the wealthy few and the masses of poor and oppressed had grown wide. While moral standards were collapsing in the public sphere, religious practices and worship of God remained very important in society.

Amos sees this contradiction clearly and judges the nation accordingly; God sees through the religious hypocrisy and condemns any unjust political-economic order that tramples on the poor. Amos warns the people of the nation that if they want to live, "hate evil and love good, and establish justice in the gate" (5:15 NRSV).

More than 140 million people are poor or low income in the United States, while a few billionaires and a cadre of millionaires hoard increasing amounts of wealth. The wealthy elite in the twenty-first century are not that different from those against whom Amos brought judgment. Both groups believe their own lies of entitlement and exceptionalism; both manipulate and control a political-economic order rooted in corruption and oppression for their own benefit; and both engage in religious worship that claims this is all God's divine order.

Evils of economic exploitation, structural racism, militarism, and Christian nationalism threaten the whole of society. These evils rely on an unholy alliance between corporate business interests, political structures, and a distorted religious narrative. We must call out against them as Amos did, proclaiming a God who stands with the poor and those who suffer from the empire's way of domination and violence.

In chapter 5, Amos begins a lament, or cry of sorrow, against this way of life: "There will be wailing in all the streets" (5:16). In our own day, the prophet Callie Greer, who lives in Selma, Alabama, and organizes with the Poor People's Campaign, tells the nation, "You must let me wail." In February 2020, she testified to her pain and oppression at a public gathering in Selma: years earlier, her daughter had died in her arms due to poverty and lack of health care. Callie cried out, "You must let me wail for the children I've lost to poverty and will never get back, wail for all the children we mothers have lost. I won't waste my pain. I hope I make you feel uncomfortable. I hope I make you feel angry. I'm wailing because my babies are no more."

In a 1967 message entitled "Where Do We Go from Here?" Rev. Dr. Martin Luther King Jr. called on the prophet Amos: "We must honestly face the fact that the movement must address itself to the question of restructuring the whole of American society," he said. The task before us is to communicate and lament "with a divine dissatisfaction."

Callie and Martin, like Amos, are speaking for God using the poetry and prophecy of lament. They are calling for justice to be worked and lived out in order to build a different world, a beloved community.

If we are not to become or remain "moral monsters," as James Baldwin described, we must remember the call of Amos. We must learn to take up the voice and struggle of the prophets today, following leaders like Callie who point the way.

— REFLECT —

What is breaking your heart? What is breaking God's heart? Please wail. Write and share your own lament or divine dissatisfaction.

— READ —

Jeremiah 31:15. Unnecessary loss is the consequence of moral and unjust disordering. This verse gives a glimpse into how we articulate the pain and suffering.

— PRAY —

Oh God of justice, let us all be dissatisfied until the United States no longer only talks about life, liberty, and freedom but actually lives out justice in the public square. Amen.

13

PRAY FOR THE DEAD, FIGHT FOR THE LIVING

Erica N. Williams

"Pray for the dead and fight like hell for the living."

—MARY HARRIS "MOTHER" JONES

READ: MATTHEW 28

On a dreary, hot day in June, I received the phone call that I had been dreading for months. Amos Jones, my dear friend and comrade in the struggle for justice, had died at the age of thirty-five because he didn't have access to quality health care.

Amos had been diagnosed with a heart condition the year before. Proper treatment would have allowed him to live longer. Unfortunately, Amos lost his job because he was no longer able to work due to his illness. As a result, his health insurance was cut. The health care that Amos had before losing his job was not adequate due to its high copays and the fact that insurance didn't cover most conditions. He was a patient at the Janes Street Community Clinic in Saginaw, Michigan, which serves the poor and marginalized. The staff did all they could to help Amos, but he was in dire need of more services than they could provide. I and the rest of Amos's village did all we could to support him, but our efforts fell short. Amos died in the midst of the fight for his freedom. What made me incredibly angry was the audacity of the people who claimed that it was Amos's time to die, that he had served his purpose. In fact, the doctors say if he had been able to have a major surgery, it would have stopped the progression of the condition.

The same summer Amos died, the Senate, led by Mitch McConnell (R-KY), proposed a bill to repeal and replace the Affordable Care Act. This bill proposed to leave an additional twenty-two million people without health insurance and allow for more drastic cuts to Medicaid in the future. There were already millions of Americans who did not have health care. To think the richest country in the world would even consider letting more people die at the hands of capitalism—well, it made me want to do things that I knew would get me locked up for a long time.

As I contemplated how to get justice for my friend, I remembered the words of Mother Jones. And I committed myself to fighting like hell for those who are living in the American Nightmare.

With Amos's story deep in my heart, I joined ten clergy from several faiths in civil disobedience against the empire's repeal-and-replace bill at Mitch McConnell's office in Washington, DC. The clergy included Rev. Dr. William J. Barber II and Rev. Dr. Liz Theoharis, cochairs of the Poor People's Campaign: A National Call for Moral Revival. We declared that health care is a human right and that every person carries the *imago Dei* (image of God). I had tears in my eyes as we called the names of those who had died because they did not have health care. I could feel Amos cheering us on, telling me to give them hell for all they had done to him and countless others.

The protest reminded me of Matthew 28, when the women go to the tomb looking for Jesus. They do not find him, because he has risen and is off continuing the work he started. Jesus's work is now empowering the disciples to fight against the empire and to know with deep confidence that he will be with them always, even unto the end of the world. Jesus also proclaims to the disciples that all authority in heaven and earth has been given to him and them. The disciples, and all those who take up the message of the good news, will have the power of the Christ consciousness to fight against the wickedness of the empire.

This chapter from Matthew pushes us to remember those who have died in the fight for freedom and to know that they never leave us. I know that Jesus and Amos were with us as we fought for universal health care in DC. I know that family members from the Poor People's Campaign who have died because of the greed of this nation are with us as we fight to change the heart and soul of this nation. I honor and remember the lives of Pamela Sue Rush, Venus Greer, Ezzard Charles "Dread" McCall, and countless others who have fought like hell against the system of injustice.

May we all be ignited with holy fire to fight like hell until the poor and dispossessed all over the globe have the dignity and basic necessities they deserve. I am committed to fighting until I give my last breath. Even then, I plan to leave this world declaring, "Give them hell until justice runs down like a mighty stream."

— REFLECT —

What are some ways you can fight for the living while honoring those who have died in the fight for freedom?

— READ —

Micah 6. The prophet shares the reason that God has a case against the people, naming ways to fight for course correction towards justice, mercy, and discipleship, in the face of deadly consequences otherwise.

— PRAY —

Creator, mold in us the mindset of "Mother" Jones, who professed, "I am not afraid of the pen, or the scaffold, or the sword. I will tell the truth wherever I please." Let us fight for justice until it rolls down like a mighty stream. Ashe and amen.

14

WAKE UP, JONAH

Karenna Gore

"And so the mother in me asks 'what if?' What if this darkness is not the darkness of the tomb, but the darkness of the womb? What if our America is not dead but is a country waiting to be born?"

—VALERIE KAUR

READ: JONAH 2:1-10

The book of Jonah begins with God's instruction to a reluctant, evasive, and frustrated prophet: go warn the people of Nineveh that God has taken notice of their wickedness. Instead, Jonah runs away, stowing away on a ship bound for Tarshish. "But the Lord hurled a great wind upon the sea," the writer tells us, creating a mighty storm (1:4 NRSV). While the other mariners pray to their gods, Jonah goes into the hold of the ship and falls asleep. They find him, wake him, and question him. He admits who he is and advises them to throw him overboard. As Jonah descends into the deep, God provides a fish to swallow him. In this passage, Jonah prays from the belly of the fish—what he calls the *sheol* ("dark land of the dead").

The great Jewish philosopher and social justice activist Abraham Joshua Heschel taught that the prophets of the Hebrew Bible give us the God's-eye view of the world. Most people see things according to measures that the powerful devise: the stock market, the gross domestic product, simplistic jobs reports. The systems causing the climate crisis are justified by these metrics. These systems are as legal and accepted as the wicked ways of the people of Nineveh. Our own tendency to flee from responsibility to change these systems is as mundane as Jonah's instinct to get on the ship and fall asleep in the hold.

But this passage shows us that God works with flawed messengers and uses human error to generate another chance at redemption. It also demonstrates what can happen when we turn toward God—often at the same time that things get so bad it feels like the darkness of the tomb. In this passage, Jonah prays: "the waters closed in over me; the deep surrounded me; weeds were wrapped around my head at the roots of the mountains. I went down to the land whose bars closed upon me forever; yet you brought up my life from the Pit" (2:5–6 NRSV).

Three days and three nights later, the giant fish spews Jonah up onto land. This is often taken as foreshadowing Jesus's own resurrection, not least because of Jesus's words in Matthew 12:38–40: "For as Jonah was three days and three nights in the belly of a huge fish, so the Son of Man will be three days and three nights in the heart of the earth." What does this signify? As activist Valarie Kaur has so powerfully spoken—including at a thrilling Watch Night service of the Poor People's Campaign in 2016—the darkness of the tomb may instead be the darkness of the womb: that sacred place of transformation before birth. The key to making it so is our own shift in perception and our reaching for the divine.

Those on the front lines of ecological devastation are bringing prophetic voice to our climate crisis. I witnessed this in Union Hill, Virginia, where people came together across race and religion to resist the build-out of the fossil fuel empire in their own community. Even in the moments of despair—as corporate power infiltrated everywhere, money was held out as paramount, and impending devastation seemed inevitable—they marched, they rallied, and they supported one another. And they prevailed! They helped to stop the construction of a vast pipeline being built in their backyards and reminded us that every struggle is an integral piece of a global constellation of freedom struggles. From the Gulf Coast to the Arctic to the Great Plains and beyond, communities need our support as they care for the earth.

The book of Jonah shows us a web of life that is divinely infused. God speaks with and through the wind, water, fish, and, later in the story, bush, worm, and scorching heat. Creation is full of agency, vitality, holiness, and divine message. It is as powerful as a womb, ever quickening and life giving.

In this prayer in Jonah 2, we find the key to responding to ecological devastation today. In these words, we learn to reject the illusion of escape, align ourselves with the divine, and step forward to do the sacred work to which we are called.

— REFLECT —

What vain idols do people worship today? Who and what do they sacrifice to these idols? How can we look to nature for signs of God's will? How are we called to respond?

— READ —

Romans 8:22. The story and prayer of Jonah remind us that in darkness, turning to God brings new identity and ushers in new life. The Romans text reminds us that all creation groans, awaiting our steps toward the divine.

— PRAY —

Divine Creator, we ask that you be with us in this moment of pain and despair and help us to see it through your eyes. Give us the strength to relinquish our illusions and our hesitation. Help us to hear the cries of those who are suffering from ecological devastation and join with them to transform the ways of the world so that the whole community of life may thrive for generations to come. Amen.

15

WE ARE NOT TRACTORS

Liz Theoharis

"What does the cry of the poor express, if not their suffering and their solitude, their disappointment and their hope? . . . We are called to make a serious examination of conscience, to see if we are truly capable of hearing the cry of the poor."

—POPE FRANCIS

READ: JAMES 5:1-6

No somos tractors; somos seres humanos. "We are not tractors; we are human beings."

In the first general strike I participated in with the Coalition of Immokalee Workers in southeast Florida, hundreds of workers held signs proclaiming the dignity of the human beings who pick the food that comes to our tables, restaurants, and grocery stores. Marching through the community, farmworkers passed by the houses and trailers of crew leaders, not far from the large farms where landowners get rich off the poverty wages they pay their workers. They marched to the parking lot where buses pick up day laborers early each morning. Asserting their humanity as they carried cardboard cutouts of tractors, these migrant workers—mainly of Guatemalan, Mexican, and Haitian descent—demanded fair wages, quality housing and working conditions, and dignity for all.

The Coalition of Immokalee Workers (CIW) was formed in 1993 by farmworkers who were being paid subpoverty wages for hard manual work and facing deplorable conditions. Since then, the CIW has identified and helped to break up seven agricultural slave labor rings in their area of the South and has brought attention to two more indentured servitude rings. In 2005, the CIW won the first raise for farmworkers in southwest Florida in thirty years, nearly doubling wages. They forced the fast-food industry, a major buyer of the tomatoes they pick, to take responsibility for the low wages and inhumane conditions in their supply chain.

Activists with the CIW have captured the imagination of tens of thousands of people and educated so many on the power and potential of undocumented, low-wage workers to lead a massive movement. This formerly unknown group of migrant laborers from an obscure part of Florida has launched a credible challenge to more than a dozen multibillion-dollar corporations. As a result of their organizing, fourteen of these corporations have signed on to the CIW's Fair Food Program.

All of this organizing and all of these victories begin with low-wage workers crying out for justice. Together, they name the immorality of their working conditions and declare that their poverty is not the will of God. Those without the "proper" papers or language, assumed to be too busy trying to survive or perceived as not powerful enough to lead: these workers are building unity and organization. They are David taking on the Goliaths of the fast-food industry.

And they are not alone in their assertion that God hears the cries of workers; they are in line with the prophets of our sacred texts, who call to account those who use their wealth and power to hurt the oppressed and rejected. The Bible preaches judgment against rich people who exploit the poor. "All the workers you've exploited and cheated cry out for judgment," writes James. "The groans of the workers you used and abused are a roar in the ears of the Master Avenger" (James 5:4 MSG).

Poverty is not inevitable, and low wages are not the will of God. Paying poverty wages is a systemic sin. Powerful low-wage workers from Immokalee and fields and farms across this country are working with faith leaders and people of conscience to denounce such practices and organize to end them.

The workers of the CIW are leading the way to social transformation; they are not waiting for politicians, policymakers, doctors, or lawyers to save them. As Frederick Douglass often noted, those in pain know when their pain is relieved, and those who would be free must strike the first blow. The Coalition of Immokalee Workers is striking that blow. Its members are crying out, and in their cries can be heard the message of a powerful song by theomusicologist Yara Allen from the Poor People's Campaign: "Somebody is hurting my brother, my sister, our workers, our children and it has gone on far too long and we won't be silent anymore."

— REFLECT —

Have you ever cried out to God for help and justice? What struggles are you aware of where injustice gets too great and the people have to cry out?

— READ —

Psalm 34:7. God's ears hear the cries of the poor, and God moves to save.

— PRAY —

Let us believe in a God who identifies with the least of these. A God of love and of abundant life who stands on the side of justice. A God who is with us in the fields of Immokalee, in the tent encampments of the unhoused in Aberdeen, and with the mothers in Flint without clean water. A God who walks with us on the picket lines and in our organizing work. Let us remember the strength and love of those unsung saints of yesterday and today who resist and lead us all to freedom. Amen.

16

WHAT WILL YOU LIFT UP?

Letiah Fraser

> "The conspicuous absence of the lynching tree in American theological discourse and preaching is profoundly revealing, especially since the crucifixion was clearly a first-century lynching."
>
> **—JAMES H. CONE**

READ: JOHN 19:16-30

George Floyd, Breonna Taylor, Botham Jean, Philando Castile, Alton Sterling, Freddie Gray, Tamir Rice, Michael Brown, Eric Garner: these bodies and names make up just a partial list of the twenty-first-century lynchings of people of color carried out by police officers and sanctioned by the state. I carry these stolen lives with me every day, as so many of us do. A friend of mine has written their names on a sticky note on a wall in her dining room. Soon she will need another one.

Meanwhile, institutional white churches continue to remain silent. Dear Christian, church member, religious leader, or moral guide: your silence perpetuates violence against the bodies of BIPOC (Black, Indigenous, and people of color) folx. Silence is complicity.

Jesus lifts up the struggles of the poor and dispossessed. A woman named Mary, living in a patriarchal society in which women were considered property, is chosen to be the bearer of the good news. Nine months later, Mary and Joseph are a homeless couple whose only access to shelter is a stable. Where will the unhoused safely live? Jesus lifts up the plight of the homeless.

As an infant, Jesus and his parents become refugees fleeing their home for Egypt. They seek asylum from a corrupt government and death threats. Jesus lifts up the plight of immigrants.

As an adult, Jesus becomes an organizer. He wants to shift the distorted, nationalistic religious narrative of his country and the world. He organizes those who are poor (including fishermen and sex workers) alongside those who have more wealth (like doctors and tax collectors). The society he lives in is set up to divide people against one another based on religion, class, gender, and ethnicity. Jesus's mission is to unite them. He announces it loud and clear in the synagogue: "The Spirit of the Lord is on me, because he has anointed me to proclaim good news to the poor" (Luke 4:18).

Jesus teaches his group of organizers the importance of caring for the poor. He shows them how to engage in projects of survival. He starts a feeding program with a little boy's lunch. He finds solidarity in the homes of friends like Mary and Martha. In the days of the coronavirus pandemic, workers who are fighting for $15 an hour and unions are leading similar projects of survival. I hope we don't cast lots for their clothes when many of them get sick and die.

Jesus and his group of organizers understand that health care is a human right. Jesus is a health care worker who puts his life on the line by offering medical care to those deemed contagious. A woman with bleeding problems, lepers, and those with disabilities are given free medical care.

At Jesus's crucifixion, the curtain of the temple—a divider that separates those who aren't permitted to enter from those who have the proper credentials—is torn in two. Jesus's crucifixion is a result of unjust government policies. Will we continue to allow unfair government policies to lead to the capital punishment of innocent people? Pilate cannot wash his hands of Jesus's blood; if we remain silent, we won't be able to wash our hands of theirs.

As Jesus hangs on the cross, darkness covers the earth. Our very ecosystem is affected by the disregard of human life. On the cross, Jesus says, "I thirst." He joins the cries of those without access to clean water, in the United States and around the world.

Jesus lifts up the cries of the poor until his last breath. He proclaims "It is finished" not because the demands of the poor have been met but because in his living, his feeding, his healing, and his organizing, he has demonstrated that society can be restructured. He has shown that we can honor the dignity and the *imago Dei*, the image of God, in every human being.

Like many leaders who came after him, Jesus was murdered because he disrupted the structures of society with an ethic of love. What he stood for did not mesh with state values. His life didn't matter to the state, which felt it had to take it as a matter of instruction to the people. Jesus becomes "strange fruit," as Billie Holiday sings in that mournful song by Abel Meeropol, hanging on the lynching tree.

When Jesus says "It is finished," he is speaking to us. Dear Christian, church member, religious leader, or moral guide: he is calling you to lay down your excuses and lift up the cry of justice.

— REFLECT —

What does this passage reveal about the devaluing of the lives of workers and BIPOC individuals? How are you working with those in your communities to dismantle systems of injustice?

— READ —

Isaiah 61:1–4. Jesus quotes the Hebrew Scriptures as a model for pursuing justice. It is for his values and actions that he is executed by the state but raised up by God.

— PRAY —

Continuously crucified God, remind us that you stand in solidarity with those whose bodies are being mutilated by systems designed to break open our bodies. Give wisdom, creativity, and courage to workers, caregivers, and those working to dismantle structural racism wherever it is found. Amen.

17

HOW BREAD CAN DIVIDE OR DIGNIFY

Melanie Mullen

"Yet what greater defeat could we suffer than to come to resemble the forces we oppose in their disrespect for human dignity?"

—RUTH BADER GINSBURG

READ: 1 CORINTHIANS 11:17-26

The ancient church of Corinth is in conflict over breaking bread. When Paul visits the new church, he writes that there is something wrong in how they come together for table fellowship. Their way of breaking bread differs from what Jesus meant to teach and pass on.

Although the Corinthians show up to dine in common, "each one shapes it according to his or her likes and enjoyment, and they fail to share with one another, as each one goes ahead with his own meal" (11:20–21, author translation). What they are doing at the celebration of the Lord's Supper only makes them *look* like they are being a community. In truth, their meal has become an occasion for social discrimination and divisive conduct.

The new church seems well-meaning on the surface, but they shame the poor in the community in the way they live out their differences. By marking the haves from the have-nots, they label each other and replicate the Roman Empire's unequal structures and emphasis on status.

Paul objects to these labels and the way they justify unfair treatment among people—unfair treatment that is remedied by remembering Jesus's example of communion meals that never make people ashamed of being poor.

Paul's letter urges the Corinthian church to remember that communion makes them a type of family, "baptized together" in the liberation of the exodus from Egypt. That first communion, taken by the Hebrew people in the desert, was a lesson in equality. Everyone who wandered in the desert was fed with God's free "bread." Paul's letter urges the Corinthians back to this vision of God's communion. It corrects their focus, reminding them that there is a purpose to the food they share: the righting of wrong relationships.

In ancient churches, bringing gifts to the table was a sacred and life-giving act. The early Christians even gathered in what were called "meals of dissent." People blessed the food and ate together, knowing that it was real communion only as long as each offering was received as an equal gift. The giver's income or background did not matter.

Thousands of years later, inside the largest laundromat in East Richmond, Virginia, a community of women lived into a shared vision of justice over a common meal like the ancient church in Corinth did. For months, a mission group from a wealthy downtown church conducted an experiment in proximity, adopting the laundromat across from Virginia's largest public housing community and giving out free quarters and snacks. These Saturday community sessions brought about feelings of joy, mutual learning, and much-needed relief for overburdened residents.

Although the church members came to give charity, the neighborhood mothers ended up sharing wisdom with them and building mutuality. The mothers taught those coming to minister to them how hard it is to sustain a family in a community shaped by decades of segregation, housing covenants, and destructive "urban renewal." They showed the mission women the impact of redlining and the nation's most biased eviction laws. They shared with them the rules against owning a clothes dryer in rental properties, even if you could pay for it. And they taught the women from the downtown church how to decide when to give up a load of clean clothes in order to afford back-to-school supplies or a child's holiday gift.

The mission project was an experiment worth celebrating. Still, when the church members wanted to host a holiday meal for the women they met in the laundromat, the East Richmond mothers first felt the need to right their new communal relationship. They changed the menu for the community Christmas party by refusing the donated snacks and insisting on bringing homemade chocolate cakes. Thus, they created a new sign and symbol through which both groups could break bread.

With their offering of chocolate cake, the Virginia mothers helped a community realize that charity without equality is dead. Rather than letting others set the agenda, they offered their own gifts and practiced right relationship instead.

Be it in Corinth or East Richmond, communities in right relationship carry on the spirit of the gospel and affirm everyone's dignity. Following the example of Jesus in breaking bread, we can each bring something to the rebalancing of community in freedom, power, love, and peace.

— REFLECT —

Paul said, "For I received from the Lord what I also passed on to you" (11:23). What have you received? What can you pass on that teaches dignity as a community practice? How do you see mutuality practiced in your community? Where is it still needed?

— READ —

Acts 6:1-7. This passage shows Jesus's disciples working toward mutuality in the early church.

— PRAY —

God who created me out of love, remind me that God loves me and I am of infinite value to God. God created me for freedom, and my freedom is inalienable and God-given. God loves me and made me for freedom. Amen.

18

WHEN IDOLS SPEAK, PEOPLE CAN'T

Michael Pollack

> "Destroying the Earth is just wrong. Hurting the poor is wrong. Treating corporations like people and people like things is just wrong."
>
> **—WILLIAM J. BARBER II**

READ: EZEKIEL 22

As long as money talks, people will never be heard. As long as idols speak, people can't.

When we headed west on foot from Thomas Paine Plaza in Philadelphia toward Harrisburg, we marched because, as Paine once wrote, "We have it in our power to begin the world over again." Ten days later, after 115 miles of praying with our feet, about sixty of us marched to the Pennsylvania State Capitol. There, we cried out against corruption in our state's marble palace and protested the greed and idolatry in this civic temple. As the prophet Ezekiel moaned, "Will you judge this city of bloodshed?"

They knew we were coming. We had already met with all but two of our 253 state legislators. We had already marched hundreds of miles, and we had already been to jail. We had already popped up at their town halls and blocked their hallways and disrupted their hearings and camped out near their houses. They knew what we demanded: pass the lobbyist gift ban, end gerrymandering, increase voting rights, make corruption illegal, and take money out of politics.

On that day, they knew our central demand was the gift ban. It should be illegal for our public officials to take bribes like expensive vacations, wining and dining, and cash gifts. We need a gift ban in Pennsylvania because the words of Isaiah 2,600 years ago are still true today: "Your rulers are rebels, partners with thieves; they all love bribes and chase after gifts. They do not defend the cause of the fatherless; the widow's case does not come before them" (1:23).

Our elected officials and the political system they serve are indifferent and unresponsive because they do not see or hear our suffering. They do not see us because they are chasing after the bribes of the ruling class. As Deuteronomy commands us, "Do not accept a bribe, for a bribe blinds the eyes of the wise and twists the words of the innocent" (16:19). They are busy sacrificing our lives to idols of money and power, to idols of greed and profit.

"Their idols are silver and gold," the psalmist writes. These idols do not speak, they do not see, they do not hear, they do not smell, and they do not feel. "Those who make them will be like them, and so will all who trust in them" (Psalm 115:4–8). As the prophet Ezekiel said, "See how each of the princes of Israel who are in you uses his power to shed blood. In you they have treated father and mother with contempt; in you they have oppressed the foreigner and mistreated the fatherless and the widow. . . . In you are people who accept bribes to shed blood; you take interest and make a profit from the poor. You extort unjust gain from your neighbors. And you have forgotten me" (22:6–7; 12).

We marched past the police outpost and around the capitol, where we assembled near a fountain. We gave speeches for no other reason than to stall until the appointed time. When the time came, eight of us moved toward the building and blocked its entrance, with dollar bills marked Bribe taped over our mouths and a banner reading Money Silences Us hanging over our heads. The Capitol Police quickly moved in and made eight arrests. At 1:05 p.m.—at the exact moment the police were escorting us to their station near the cafeteria and the legislature was pledging allegiance at the beginning of their session—we dropped $500 in $1 bills marked BRIBE onto the House floor. As the money fluttered down, we unfurled a banner emblazoned first with words of Rabbi Heschel: "Some are guilty, all are responsible." This was followed by one that read "Pass the gift ban now!"

Hours later, we walked out of jail to the news that the speaker of the House had cosponsored the gift ban and was in full support of passing it.

Our elected officials stray after idols; the system they prop up is built upon the worship of false idols like money, power, and fame. It pretends to be dedicated to helping all people thrive, but in reality it works to benefit the few at the expense of the many. It is a system of corrupt indifference that is killing us. It follows the golden rule of the golden idols: "The guy with the gold makes the rules."

May we instead follow the actual golden rule: "Love your neighbor as yourself" (Leviticus 19:18).

— REFLECT —

Think about how bribery and corruption have affected your community. What feelings come up? Where do you see hope? How can you participate with others to reclaim your voice?

— READ —

Deuteronomy 16:18–22. This passage continues to expose the insidious nature of bribery and makes clear that officials must pursue justice only.

— PRAY —

As we give our lives to a movement of justice, may you bless us and protect us, may your face turn toward us and be gracious toward us, may your face shine upon us, and may there be peace. God of history, may we have the courage and the strength to move you from your throne of justice and wrath to your throne of mercy and love. Amen.

19

NABOTH'S VINEYARD AND THE STRUGGLE FOR OAK FLAT

Adam Barnes

"If you want to learn how to be in this world, you must go to the places that suffer. Then listen and learn there."

—WENDSLER NOSIE SR.

READ: 1 KINGS 21

Oak Flat, known to the Apache as Chi'chil Bildagoteel, is about sixty miles outside of Phoenix, Arizona. It is just east of Apache Leap, a sheer cliff where, in the late nineteenth century, seventy-five Apache warriors jumped to their deaths rather than be captured by a pursuing US cavalry.

Apache have lived at Chi'chil Bildagoteel since the beginning of time as they remember it. Usen, the Creator, created and placed the Ga'an at Chi'chil Bildagoteel as a blessing for the Apache. It is comparable to Mount Sinai, where Christians and Jews believe Moses received God's promise and came to know God's will for how humans should live in this world. The Apache believe that *Ga'an*, or spirits, reside at Chi'chil

Bildagoteel. Generations of Apache girls have had their coming-of-age ceremonies there, and people gather acorns and harvest medicinal plants there. It is a place of beauty and abundance, where the Apache honor and offer prayers to the Creator and to their ancestors. This is where Apache come to the corridor to connect with the Ga'an to remember who they are.

More than a mile below the ground in Oak Flat is one of the largest copper deposits in North America. Many Apache, for whom this land is sacred, are not surprised that there is such an abundance of precious resources beneath the ground. They are also not surprised that multinational mining companies Rio Tinto and BHP Billiton and their joint venture, Resolution Copper, seek to extract the copper and destroy Oak Flat in the process. Wendsler Nosie Sr., founder of Apache Stronghold, is leading a fight against the land's desecration. He explains what is at stake in that fight: "They have declared war on our religion. We must stand in unity and fight to the very end, for this is a holy war."

The desire to dominate people and possess land and resources is an ancient story. King Ahab once coveted the land of a small native farmer named Naboth. "Let me have your vineyard to use for a vegetable garden, since it is close to my palace," Ahab says (21:2). He offers Naboth money for the land, but Naboth refuses: "The Lord forbid that I should give you the inheritance of my ancestors" (21:3). Ahab becomes angry and sullen at Naboth's refusal. With the help of his wife, Jezebel, Ahab plots to take Naboth's land and has him discredited and killed.

When Naboth refuses to sell his ancestral land, it is not only a challenge to the authority of the king but also an appeal to a different moral authority, a different God. The God who Naboth obeys—and who Ahab betrays—is clear that land is a blessing to all and not to be possessed by anyone. Caring for the land is part of how we care for our relationship with each other, with the earth, with our ancestors, and ultimately with God. Put simply, land is sacred. It binds Naboth to those who came before him and forms the basis of his relationship to God. It is not Naboth's land but God's, and therefore not Naboth's to sell. Ahab has lost sight of this; he has been seduced by the illusion of a false god that leads him to believe he can possess the land, and in so doing gain control over life itself.

When Wendsler and Apache Stronghold rejected Resolution Copper's various offers and threats to mine Oak Flat, they, like Naboth, not only rejected the company and its greed; they rejected the whole system of beliefs and practices to which these powerbrokers are obedient. Wendsler and the other Apache affirm a different way of being in the world—a different way of walking with God.

King Ahab eventually repents and is redeemed. It is hard to imagine Resolution Copper or any other giant multinational mining company doing the same today. Yet Ahab's redemption reminds us that it is not Ahab the person who God condemned. Naboth saw what Wendsler and the Apache so clearly see today: their fight is not against the people who covet holy land but against a false god that compels people to covet, possess, and ultimately destroy God's creation.

In these times, we must confront these systems that covet land and seek God-like power over life and death. And to do this we will need to continue to look for leadership in those places where the rejected live and fight. If we are to win, we must listen to, learn from, and unite our struggle with Wendsler, the Apache, and the many other prophetic leaders and communities across the country and world fighting to defend that which is sacred.

— REFLECT —

What does it mean for land to be sacred? Who gets to define what is sacred? Why? How does the land connect you with your community, past and present, and with God?

— READ —

Genesis 1:1-31. Reflect on how much emphasis is placed on all life being created with inherent goodness.

— PRAY —

God of creation and abundant life, of death and rebirth, we give thanks for this good earth. Help us see the goodness in all life and reject the forces that degrade life. Amen.

PART III
THE DAYS OF LIBERATION

20

SHOULD WE SIT AT THE TABLE— OR TURN IT OVER?

Janelle Bruce

> "Freedom is not a state; it is an act. It is not some enchanted garden perched high on a distant plateau where we can finally sit down and rest. Freedom is the continuous action we must all take, and each generation must do its part to create an even more fair, more just society."
>
> —JOHN LEWIS

READ: MARK 11

When Jesus comes to the temple, he drives out those who are selling and buying, and he overturns the tables of the money changers. He says, "Is it not written: 'My house will be called a house of prayer for all the nations'? But you have made it a 'den of robbers.'"

Doing justice and overturning tables is not an option but a mandate. Holy disruption is a mandate for those who follow Christ, those who profess love as their religion, and those who believe in justice. While comfort leads us to accept more of the same, our faith calls us to disrupt that which harms God's people.

We cannot become so comfortable having a seat at the table that we refuse to flip it over when it becomes a tool of oppression. We cannot fail to act because we fear the consequences.

I watched the radical work of the Forward Together Moral Movement when the group's protests first began in 2013. I was awed by North Carolinians of different backgrounds standing together, with the crowd growing from dozens to hundreds to thousands, Monday after Monday. These holy disruptors fought against the destruction of voting rights, tax codes that would hurt the most vulnerable, and policies that would devastate students, the poor, the elderly, and African Americans.

Some observers considered these Moral Mondays a mere disruption. Extremists went as far as to call them "Moron Mondays." But those who marched, sang, and gathered week after week recognized that their work was holy. Their witness was so powerful that it caused me, a woman living hundreds of miles away, to quit my job at a law firm, begin divinity school, and commit to merging ministry and justice.

For far too long, churches have depoliticized the gospel of Jesus that demands love and justice in action. We hear pleas from faith leaders to separate politics from faith, to avoid protests, and to refrain from disrupting life as we know it. Simply trust God, they tell us. Yet it is puzzling that those who profess to follow a brown-skinned Palestinian Jew who boldly disrupted injustice can tell others to remain silent.

When we have fewer voting rights today than we did fifty years ago, we need holy disruption. When seven hundred people die every day from poverty in the United States while the richest amass and hoard wealth, we must engage in holy disruption. Holy disruption demands that people be treated justly and reminds our legislators that they are servant-leaders who will be held accountable to the people. If we walk in the radical nature of Christ when we step into spaces of injustice, people will think, here comes trouble: good, liberating, loving, Christlike trouble!

Moral Mondays were so successful because they were full of organized holy disrupters committed to a moral framework. After a dozen weeks, nearly a thousand people had gone to jail and twenty thousand people stood strong on Fayetteville Street in Raleigh, committed to the holy work of justice. This commitment left the nation and the media asking, "What's really happening?" The response from Bishop William Barber II to the crowd on that day was "This is the Lord's doing, and it is marvelous."

On that first Moral Monday, Jesus showed us how to overturn tables. May we remember Jesus the revolutionary, the refugee, the prisoner, and the table turner. May we embody Jesus who fought for the poor, questioned corrupt religious establishments, and challenged the evil policies of the government. Just as Jesus disrupted the Roman Empire, we are the moral witnesses of today, and we are called to disrupt the unjust empires of our time.

— REFLECT —

How was Jesus turning the tables a holy act? As civil rights leader John Lewis would say, what "good trouble" might you be called to in this season? What will you do to disrupt the sinful policies and poverty that harm the most marginalized in our society?

— READ —

Amos 5:11-15. This is a strong rebuke of those trampling and robbing the poor. How can hating evil and loving good lead to holy disruption?

— PRAY —

Lord, we commit ourselves to holy disruption today and always. May your love strengthen us to endure the good trouble necessary to liberate all of your children. May your wisdom guide us as we work to create a world full of compassion, grace, and justice—a world where love is the law of the land. Amen.

21

DON'T YOU WANT TO IMPROVE YOUR COMMUNITY?

Leonardo Vilchis

> "Even when they call us mad, when they call us subversives and communists and all the epithets they put on us, we know we only preach the subversive witness of the Beatitudes, which have turned everything upside down."
>
> —OSCAR ROMERO

READ: MATTHEW 22:15-22

After Jesus enters Jerusalem and drives the merchants out of the temple, the Pharisees try to entrap him with questions about what belongs to Caesar. Finding themselves challenged by Jesus's actions, the Pharisees in turn question his authority. These established authorities of law and order are looking for a way to entrap Jesus with his own words. But the way Jesus answers sends them away astonished.

The residents of the Pico Gardens Housing Projects in Boyle Heights, Los Angeles, have found themselves in these types of confrontations with authorities many times. Just like Jesus was, they have been pushed into entrapment. And it always comes in the form of a question: "Don't you want to improve your community?"

When Rosa and Yolanda asked the police in a community meeting to withdraw their aggressive presence from their neighborhood, elected leaders, police captains, and the media asked, "Don't you want to improve your community?" The police had been harassing the youth—detaining them unnecessarily, beating them up, and antagonizing them. At the meeting, Rosa and Yolanda asked, "How have the police decreased the crime in our neighborhood?"

The police couldn't answer.

When Manuela and Carmen opposed the demolition of their homes at a housing authority meeting of Pico Gardens and Aliso Village, developers, politicians, reporters, and local leaders asked, "Don't you want to improve your community?" After the demolition of the housing project, more than nine hundred very low-income families were displaced. At the meeting, Manuela and Carmen asked, "Is everybody going to be able to return?"

The board of commissioners stayed silent.

When Ana and Delmira opposed the proposal for an arts district in their neighborhood, artists, developers, college professors, politicians, and reporters asked, "Don't you want to improve your community?" The development of an arts district was a strategy to gentrify the neighborhood and increase land values. It would encourage the privatization of public housing that protects very low-income families, and it would promote rent increases and evictions in the neighborhood. Ana and Delmira asked the people in the room, "Is the art district going to bring back the housing we lost and lower our rents?"

The artists silently left the room, and the developers and politicians waited for each other to answer.

When the women of the projects in the community of Boyle Heights question the presence of the police in their neighborhood, the demolition of public housing projects, or development plans in their neighborhood, they are not only reacting to an imminent danger; they are also challenging an established order. In this order, authorities and experts define what is good or bad for the community. Under this established order, acquiescence is expected and celebrated.

The police, the politicians, the developers, the artists, the leaders: they all have a plan, and they are all part of an establishment that has existed for a long time. Their plan has been presented as something natural that people must accept. The experts and professionals, emanating authority, have explained and justified that order to the community. When people don't accept this order, or when they question it, the same experts and authorities make them seem crazy or ignorant.

The question "Don't you want to improve your community?" is a trap. It is meant to shame the women into accepting the imposition. It asks the community to agree to terms of development that are defined by an outside power: the police, developers, housing authorities, licensed professionals, and officials. All of them serve a state that has surrendered to the idolatry of the market and forgotten the needs of its people.

Just like Jesus did with the Pharisees, many communities question the order under which they live and the plans that others have for them. When they challenge the established order, they are confronted by authorities who maintain that order. The experts question their intelligence and seek to shame them into submission by their own words.

But like Jesus, the women of Boyle Heights question that power. It is their neighborhood; they know what is good for them. Many have lived in their neighborhood for decades and generations. Over time, they have developed an understanding of what is important, what is necessary to have a life with dignity there. Their authority comes from living in that community, from knowing each other, and from understanding what the community really needs. They don't seek to "improve" their community; they seek a life with dignity for each other. They do not render unto the police and developers but unto truth and dignity and justice for all.

— REFLECT —

What are authorities proposing for you and your community? Do those proposals meet your needs? How do we stand in solidarity with communities that question the experts and authorities? How are we part of efforts to question the knowledge and power of impacted communities? What is development or improvement when the people most affected don't have a say in it?

— READ —

Galatians 2. Status and high esteem do not justify. Exclusion and division have nothing to do with God.

— PRAY —

God, today we ask you to help us listen to and identify the voices of those who point to new directions, a new order that centers on the voice of the excluded. Help us to hear these voices and to support the new order they are bringing forth in our world today, as Jesus did and continues to do. Amen.

22

RESURRECTING HOPE

Keith M. Bullard II

> "Hope is being able to see that there is light despite all of the darkness."
>
> —DESMOND TUTU

READ: LUKE 24:1-6

At 6:00 a.m., the day is just starting and my morning routine is in full effect. After my devotional, the morning news becomes my soundtrack. It is an unrelenting reminder of our broken economy, with skyrocketing unemployment and widespread homelessness; of racial tensions pushed to a breaking point; and of the pain and desperation caused by a society that fails us at every turn.

On one particular morning, I think of a time when the people of God found hope after the death and burial of Jesus the Christ. It was what some would have called a hopeless situation. They were grieving, scared, and unsure about their future. Do you identify with this surge of emotions?

On the first day of the week after Jesus's death, very early in the morning, the women take the spices they have prepared and go to the tomb. They find the stone rolled away, but when they enter, they do not find the body of the Lord Jesus. While the women are still wondering about this, two men, in clothes that gleam like lightning, suddenly stand beside them.

In their fright, the women bow down with their faces to the ground, but the men say to them, "Why do you look for the living among the dead? He is not here: he has risen!"

The angels tell them to go and tell the disciples. This, right here, has to be the greatest news of all time. These three words are what the disciples had hoped for: "He has risen!" The disciples don't have CNN, MSNBC, or Fox News; what they do have is the faithfulness of Mary, Joanna, and others. These women are tasked with spreading hope after the resurrection. This hope means the confident expectation of what God has promised even in hard times; its strength is in God's faithfulness.

When we look back at the times when our nation needed hope, we can always find hope in people the Bible would call "the least of these": the broken bodies of America's prosperity, the essential but all-too-often-forgotten workers. We find hope in our sister Harriet Tubman, who was forcefully enslaved and broke free to spread the hope of freedom. We find hope in our sister Rosa Parks, who spread the hope of racial equality. We find hope in Rev. Dr. Martin Luther King Jr., who challenged America to be true to what it says on paper. And in our faith, we find hope in a brown-skinned Palestinian Jewish man, who was a carpenter that became the author and finisher of our faith: Jesus the Christ. Among the death, doom, gloom, and despair that dominate the airwaves, there are those who are resurrecting hope among broken bodies.

Hope is being resurrected through Chaplains on the Harbor in Washington state. They use a closed church building as a community center that provides classes, clothing, and laundry and shower facilities. They regularly visit county and municipal jails, staying in touch with so many in the community who end up in prison and reminding them that they are not alone. Hope is being resurrected through low-wage workers at the forefront of the Fight for $15 movement, which is uniting the working class with the rallying cry of "$15 an hour and a union!" During the COVID-19 pandemic, along with Carolina Jews for Justice and the Poor People's Campaign, NC Raise Up launched a political food distribution drive called Fed Up, which is stepping in to do what our government isn't by both building worker power and keeping bellies full.

The Scriptures describe how, after the crucifixion, the disciples are in hiding. They are scared, trying to make sense of things and figure out their next move. Even though they have witnessed miracle after miracle firsthand, doubt has kicked in, and hope has begun to fade.

But Mary, Joanna, and the other women continue to do what they have always done: show honor to their Lord Jesus. Despite being scared and grieving themselves, and without knowing how they will remove the stone from the tomb, they remain confident that Jesus will fulfill his promise of justice for those at the bottom.

Finding hope on your favorite news channel or website or in your favorite newspaper may be difficult. But if you take a good look, Jesus is still revealing himself and resurrecting hope all throughout the land.

— REFLECT —

Has your hope begun to fade? Where do you see hope being resurrected? Maybe it's through the Black Lives Matter chants and demands, or through workers organizing to improve things not only in their workplace but also in their communities. What efforts and organizations give you hope? What promises are you counting on God to fulfill?

— READ —

Isaiah 41:10. When hope fades, when dismay and fear set in, this verse reminds us that God's presence is always near. God remains faithful to us.

— PRAY —

Loving God, encompass all of these movements in your embrace and enable us all to dedicate ourselves to preaching, teaching, and spreading the good news: the news of hope. Amen.

23

DENIED DIGNITY IN LIFE AND IN DEATH

Liz Theoharis

"I must remind you that starving a child is violence. Suppressing a culture is violence. Neglecting school children is violence. Punishing a mother and her family is violence. Discrimination against a working man is violence. Ghetto housing is violence. Ignoring medical need is violence. Contempt for poverty is violence."

—CORETTA SCOTT KING

READ: MATTHEW 27:1-10

In New York City, there is a powerful organization made up of and led by poor and homeless people working for housing and dignity called Picture the Homeless (PTH). In 2003, PTH lost one of its cofounders to the streets. Lewis Haggins died homeless on the subway, and it was six months before his friends and family were able to learn of his death. He was buried on Hart Island, the potter's field of New York City.

Although potter's fields—also known as paupers' graves—show up in places like the musical *Les Misérables*, the movie *It's a Wonderful Life*, Johnny Cash songs, and various books and TV shows, not many know of the true brutality of such graveyards for the poor. More than a million people have been buried on Hart Island in New York City since the US Civil War, including thousands of victims of epidemics like the flu of 1918, AIDS, and COVID-19. People are buried in unidentified mass graves, with one hundred adults or one thousand children to a grave. Their families and friends have limited access, if any, to the island and no access to the actual grave site. Until recently, Hart Island was under the jurisdiction of the Department of Correction, and Rikers Island jail inmates were paid fifty cents an hour to bury the dead. Many did so with great care, because they realized that the potter's field may be where their own bodies would be left to rest. And until poor and homeless people organized, no memorial services were allowed for those buried there.

In 2004, Picture the Homeless held Lewis Haggins's memorial service in James Chapel at Union Theological Seminary. Sitting together, currently and formerly homeless leaders, clergy, friends, and other activists prayed and honored Lewis and remembered this brilliant leader. They wrote their own version of the scripture in Matthew 27, which compared their situation to the poor in the Bible. This reinterpretation and memorial service liturgy was documented in the master's thesis of Rev. Amy Gopp.

Amy: When morning came, all the chief priests and the elders of the people conferred together against Jesus in order to bring about his death.
William: Who decided that we should die?
Dawn: Was it the shelter?
Bruce: Was it the HMO?
Torrey: Was it the government?

Amy: They bound him, led him away, and handed him over to Pilate the governor.
Rogers: We were found slumped in a subway car,
Mike: We were taken by MTA,
Jean: We were handed over to NYPD,
William: Who passed us on to the medical examiner,
Dawn: Who passed us on to the Department of Correction,
Bruce: Who handed us over to Hart Island,
Torrey: Where we were buried as anonymous units in the potter's field.

Amy: When Judas, his betrayer, saw that Jesus was condemned, he repented and brought back the thirty pieces of silver to the chief priests and the elders.

Rogers: We're handed over for a whole lot more than thirty pieces of silver;

Mike: Thirty-eight thousand of us were handed over to the Department of Homeless Services for $700 million last year.

Jean: The Volunteers of America, Salvation Army, Help USA, Samaritan Village, and the Doe Fund receive these "pieces of silver"—the $700 million—from the Department of Homeless Services.

Amy: He said, "I have sinned by betraying innocent blood." But they said, "What is that to us? See to it yourself."

William: They handed us over—none of us were guilty, just poor.

Dawn: But what do they care why we became homeless?

Amy: Throwing down the pieces of silver in the temple, he departed; and he went and hanged himself.

Bruce: But we have seen no remorse in the Judases of our day;

Torrey: They fling coins into their coffers and into our coffins and carry on.

Amy: But the chief priests, taking the pieces of silver, said, "It is not lawful to put them into the treasury, since they are blood money."

Rogers: But our temples,

Mike: Citibank,

Jean: Real estate,

William: Wall Street,

Dawn: Multinational corporations,

Bruce: Won't refuse our blood money.

Amy: After conferring together, they used them to buy the potter's field as a place to bury foreigners.

Torrey: In 1868, New York City spent $75,000 to purchase Hart Island.

Rogers: This would become the final resting place for the nameless, indigent, and homeless poor.

Amy: For this reason that field has been called the Field of Blood to this day.

Mike: That is why it is called the Field of Blood to this day.

Amy: Then was fulfilled what had been spoken through the prophet Jeremiah: "And they took the thirty pieces of silver, the price of the one on whom a price had been set, on whom some of the people of Israel had set a price, and they gave them for the potter's field, as the Lord commanded me."

Jean: What's the price paid for the dignity of the dead?

Together: What's the price paid for the dignity of the living poor?

— REFLECT —

How are the lives and deaths of the poor in your community devalued?

— READ —

Zechariah 11:12–13. This is God's response to denying people dignity and worth.

— PRAY —

God who teaches us to mourn for the dead and fight like hell for the living, we lift up prayers for those who have died because of injustice and who have been buried in fields of blood. May we find peace knowing that their memories live on. And may we not rest until freedom comes. Amen.

24

WALKING OFF THE JOB TO HELP GOD

Aaron Scott

"We're fighting for the same things the sanitation workers fought for: respect and a decent wage. When the sanitation workers had their strike, they inspired other people-they showed us how to fight for better things on the job."

—ASHLEY CATHEY

READ: MATTHEW 4:12-23, JOHN 21:1-14

"At once they left their nets and followed him": Peter, Andrew, James, and John were apparently ready, at a moment's notice, to walk off the job. How bad must this job have been?

Fishing in the ancient Mediterranean was neither the safest nor the most comfortable work. Fish was a staple food across the ancient Roman Empire, consumed by all classes, and so fishing was a major industry. You had the people who caught it, the people who built the boats, the people who sold licenses and collected taxes on it, the police who cracked down on illegal fishing, the people who ran fish processing facilities, the merchants who shipped it. All of this was taking place in a society where the vast majority of people were living in poverty and barely surviving day to day. There was no "middle class" in Jesus's lifetime. There were the elites, and then there was everyone else. People who fished for a living were in that "everyone else" group.

The Bible is the most positive media we have about poor people. Where else do we hear the message that poor people like these fishermen—who are doing the dirtiest, most dangerous, most undervalued work—are chosen by God as leaders in this world? Where else do we hear the message that poor people are allowed—and even called by God—to walk off their dirty, dangerous, undervalued jobs in order to help God change the world? We don't hear that on the news. We don't read it in the newspapers. Liberal and conservative talking heads alike generally fail to see poor people as moral leaders and true authorities on how best to fix this unjust society. Yet just about every time we open the Bible, we are confronted with story after story of regular poor people stepping up to transform God's world.

In June 2018, nine religious leaders from different faiths were arrested on the steps of the Supreme Court in Washington, DC, for praying—and for refusing to disperse as they prayed—for an end to poverty and injustice. They were held overnight in jail. After they were released, Rev. Dr. Liz Theoharis and Shailly Gupta Barnes talked about their experience of being held on the women's side of the jail. Their group had spent a long time talking with other inmates, all of whom were poor women. As Shailly, Liz, and the other protestors talked about the Poor People's Campaign, which had organized the action, they shared how they had risked arrest to bring attention to the staggering rates of poverty in this wealthy nation. The other women began to tell their own stories of surviving poverty and fighting against it.

One woman was suffering from domestic abuse and was in jail because she had fought back. One had been late to work and was arrested for running a stoplight. One was a fast-food worker named Baby who didn't stick to the limits that her employer put on how much food went into each order. She knew people were coming in who couldn't afford what they needed, and so she piled on extra meatballs and toppings to their orders. No one was going to go hungry on her watch because they couldn't afford to eat.

Baby told the other women they should come into her restaurant and that other Poor People's Campaign folks should come in too, to get free or reduced-priced meals so that they could continue the fight. She wanted to help random poor people as well as support the cause of the poor organizing for justice.

What kind of leaders is God calling, right now, to spearhead the salvation of this broken and beautiful world? Those living comfortably at the top? Or those risking their very lives and livelihoods to do the right thing—to feed God's people, and to keep one another alive when the powers and principalities turn their backs on the poor? God is *always* choosing folks from the bottom to get us back on track. Why? Because people at the bottom are the ones who know how profoundly things need to change.

That's why Jesus called these four fishermen. That's who Jesus is inviting us to hear today, too: leaders from the bottom. Farmworkers. School cafeteria workers. Fast-food workers like Baby and Ashley Cathey, who has worked for Church's Chicken in Memphis for eleven years and earns $7.53 an hour.

The gospel is for all of us—God's dream is for all of us. But bridging the gap between this burning world and "earth as it is in heaven" is going to require a very particular kind of leadership.

— REFLECT —

Know that you are a chosen leader of God. In a world that is so abundant with food but full of so many hungry people, how is God calling you to act so that all can be fed?

— READ —

Malachi 3. God creates a world of abundance and considers it robbery when people lack food.

— PRAY —

God, who fills the seas with fish, the fields with grain, and the trees with ripe fruit: protect us as we fight for our birthright to abundant food on every table, every day. Amen.

25

A MIXED MULTITUDE

Daniel Jones

> "We are determined to be people. We are saying that we are God's children. And that we don't have to live like we are forced to live. Now, what does all of this mean in this great period of history? It means that we've got to stay together. We've got to stay together and maintain unity. You know, whenever Pharaoh wanted to prolong the period of slavery in Egypt, he had a favorite, favorite formula for doing it. What was that? He kept the slaves fighting among themselves. But whenever the slaves get together, something happens in Pharaoh's court, and he cannot hold the slaves in slavery. When the slaves get together, that's the beginning of getting out of slavery. Now let us maintain unity."
>
> —MARTIN LUTHER KING JR.

READ: EXODUS 12:33-42

Many people are familiar with the stories in Exodus, the biblical book that recounts the liberation of the ancient Israelites from slavery and oppression under Pharaoh's empire. Today, when it seems like there will be no end to evil and oppression, we draw lessons and inspiration from these stories. In them we see the power of God is a power that liberates from oppression.

In this ancient story, the people were leaving an empire whose power would be broken by its contempt for God and humanity. It was an empire based on violence and injustice that sacrificed lives to the accumulation of wealth and, in its paranoia, viewed the murder of children as a fair price for keeping control. The Israelites, with a prophetic clarity born of facing the worst of this system, saw that there was no way to achieve peace or justice under Pharaoh. They began to organize and demand the freedom to remake society. Many of us turn to the exodus story for strength.

But a tiny and often overlooked verse in Exodus opens up the story of freedom even wider. When the Israelites made their break for freedom, the Bible says that they went out not by themselves but, as many translations say, with a "mixed multitude." This Scripture suggests to us that it wasn't only the Israelites who suffered under the empire. When they initiated a struggle for freedom, other poor, exploited, and suffering people in Pharaoh's empire rallied along with them. This "mixed multitude" was the group that marched to the sea, moving along the seemingly impossible path to freedom.

The Hebrew word used in Exodus 12:38 to describe this "mixture" is *erev*. It's an uncommon word, used only twice in this same way, in all of the Hebrew Bible, to describe a group of people. Variations of the term show up most often in Leviticus, where it's used to describe the horizontal threads in a woven cloth, as opposed to the vertical threads. Taken together, these two senses of the word draw a powerful metaphor for shared struggle that weaves together diverse groups to create a whole greater and stronger than its parts.

This mixed multitude came together at the bottom of the imperial hierarchy, across ethnic, cultural, and even religious boundaries. Together, they seized on the weakness of an empire weighed down by its own injustice. They took the opportunity to weave a new and better society, not according to the whims of Pharaoh but according to the law and will of God. This higher law proclaims the accumulation of individual wealth to be immoral and demands freedom for enslaved people, forgiveness of debts, care for the environment, and the responsibility of everyone to their neighbors.

This tradition continues to speak clearly to us, thousands of years later. Today, people are crying out to God against evictions, unemployment, low wages, homelessness, the violence of police and courts and jails, the denial of health care, the separation of families, hunger, and more. And although the weight of suffering is tremendous, it is possible for us to move out from under it. Today, as in Exodus, the only way out from under oppression is to move in shared struggle. Our fusion is God's instrument of liberation. God's power is made manifest when diverse peoples discover their unity, strengthen it, and act as one to end and replace a hurtful system.

People are getting together at the bottom and forging a unity that our modern pharaohs would have us believe is undesirable or impossible or both. When we speak and act with prophetic clarity, a mixed multitude starts to rally: a new mixed multitude to reorganize society. The will of God is in this unity. The mighty hand and the outstretched arm of God (Exodus 6:6) emerge from this unity. And it will deliver us from bondage again today.

— REFLECT —

What "mixed multitude" are you grateful for? What mixed multitude do you hope for? What freedom does God want for us?

— READ —

Isaiah 56:1–8. The pursuit of God's justice, not our backgrounds or social roles, unites us.

— PRAY —

Blessed are you, Source of life and Spirit of loving freedom, who brings mixed multitudes together and breaks empires apart. Bless us today with togetherness, as you blessed the Southern Tenant Farmers' Union, the National Welfare Rights Organization, the Poor People's Campaign, the Black Panthers, and the original Rainbow Coalition. Keep us with each other in the fight for freedom. Help us feel the power you give us. Let us live in the ways you have shown us. Let us get there together. Amen.

26

THE POWER THE GROUND HOLDS

Becca Forsyth

> "Some of us who have already begun to break the silence of the night have found that the calling to speak is often a vocation of agony, but we must speak. We must speak with all the humility that is appropriate to our limited vision, but we must speak."
>
> —MARTIN LUTHER KING JR.

READ: LUKE 19:28-44

I used to lie awake at night and listen to the cries of my city: the wail of the sirens as ambulances responded to the wounded. I could feel the pain in the mourning of mothers who have had to bury their sons and daughters, the cry of children who have not been fed, the fear of those who live in threat of violence every day. The newspaper was filled with stories of those who had overdosed on drugs or stolen bread to eat. I watched my friend's eight-year-old child die of leukemia. I could feel the terror other friends felt when they returned from battlefields on the other side of the world after seeing unbelievable violence condoned and conducted by our own government. Our country hires our poor to kill their poor.

As my fear and rage grew, I could also hear the whimpers of the land, contaminated by waste and greed. Not only do humans do unbelievable damage to humans, but we are also killing Mother Earth. I could feel the roar of the water, polluted and robbed of its life-giving strength. I could feel the sludge flowing in the rivers and the anguish of the fish it was killing. I was unable to catch my breath as the air we breathe was choked by emissions. I could feel the suffering of the earth as we injected fracking chemicals into her.

I felt trapped—as if someone had constructed a giant, invisible web that was trapping us all. It seemed that injustice and inequality were everywhere I looked.

As Jesus entered Jerusalem one week before the end of his earthly ministry, he was surrounded by crowds cheering "Blessed is the king who comes in the name of the Lord!" The religious scholars of that day saw this as heresy and bit back at Jesus to quiet his followers. Jesus heard this cacophony, saw the imperial guard entering the city from the other side, and contemplated the poverty and evil oppressing his people. He responded, "If they keep quiet, the stones will cry out!"

Perhaps he was referring to the power the ground holds when it absorbs that much pain and misery. What if the earth can't help but feel as we feel? If we aren't compelled to cry out, perhaps the planet herself will have to mourn.

For a time, all this pain kept me locked, unable to understand the connectedness of these stories. I saw each as a separate grief. Once I discovered the Poor People's Campaign, I quickly learned about the pattern embedded within it all. These incidents were inextricably interwoven with the evils of systemic racism, poverty, the war economy, and ecological devastation. I learned that those in power create false moral narratives that tell us that we get what we deserve and that if we don't have enough to survive, it's our fault. I saw how my neighbors were not disconnected people with faulty processors, but insects caught in this web.

That was when I decided that I had to become an organizer, an ally, a freedom fighter. I had to help my brothers and sisters break free of the tyranny all around us. I didn't know what else to do but cry out in the loudest voice I could muster: *Everybody's got a right to live!* I started to scream, until I realized that there were more folks joining the movement.

The more we screamed, the more my friends joined us. Maybe I wasn't out here alone! Maybe, just maybe, there were other folks who cared just as deeply. Maybe they were moved by their own pain and by the pain the ground had absorbed, just like I was. Maybe the power of that pain was so strong that it moved us to action and is continuing to make us cry out. Those cries create the conditions for change.

Jesus came into Jerusalem with a nonviolent army of the poor crying out for change. The established leaders refused to hear those cries and tried to silence them, thinking if they killed the movement leader, the movement itself would end. But that movement grew, and this movement grows. We have been given this amazing land of abundance, and I refuse to believe the lies of scarcity. Instead, I will speak out with my movement family. We won't be silent anymore!

— REFLECT —

What pain do you see in our world that refuses to be silent and instead cries out to God? How are the established leaders reacting to voiced pain? How do those reactions impact you? What will help you and your movement family to continue crying out?

— READ —

Matthew 5:1–13. In the Sermon on the Mount, Jesus tells us that the 140 million poor and low-income people in America are blessed and will inherit the kingdom of heaven. If we were all made in the image of God, then we all have a right to a piece of the pie. The poor will inherit the earth; has the time come to claim our inheritance?

— PRAY —

Holy Creator, you breathed the breath of life and love into each and every creature on this planet. Help us to remember that we were designed to be together in love, not against each other in hate. Let us speak into reality your peace and heal this land of abundance that you have provided for us. Amen.

27

WHEN WOMEN TESTIFY, THINGS CHANGE

Tejai Beulah

"All of this is on account of we want to register, to become first-class citizens. And if the Freedom Democratic Party is not seated . . . I question America. Is this America, the land of the free and the home of the brave, where we have to sleep with our telephones off the hooks because our lives be threatened daily, because we want to live as decent human beings, in America?"

—FANNIE LOU HAMER

READ: JOHN 20:1-18

What happens when poor and marginalized women testify about their lives? What happens when poor and marginalized women lead?

Early Western church historians have significantly downplayed the importance of Mary Magdalene in the story of Christianity. John 20:1–18 demonstrates that this woman is the first of Jesus's disciples to see him and to have a conversation with him after the resurrection. Mary discovers the empty tomb. Jesus addresses Mary. Mary testifies about her encounter with Jesus to his male disciples.

Rather than praising Mary's role in the resurrection story, historians have presented her as a "prostitute" who could be dismissed in Jesus's biography. Perhaps, this portrayal came about to lessen the discomfort of early male church leaders who could not fathom a woman's authority within the religion. Yet Mary plays an active role in Jesus's ministry. Not only does Jesus heal Mary; Mary financially supports him. She is the first to see him after he rises from the dead, and she is the first to proclaim "I have seen the Lord," as well as to detail Jesus's pending ascension.

Mary's testimony undoubtedly sets off the work of those male disciples, who go on to become evangelists and produce letters included in the New Testament. When Mary shares the story of her experience with Christ, a major world religion is born.

What is even more significant about Mary Magdalene's role in Jesus's life is that she and several other women represent that Jesus valued diversity, inclusivity, and equity in his movement. Early Christian interpreters did not fully share Jesus's values around empowering women, and many still do not today. Many Christian denominations still do not ordain women. Nevertheless, Mary Magdalene's life and testimony demonstrate that Jesus valued and included female leaders in his ministry.

Where Mary Magdalene's testimony pioneered the creation of Christianity, Fannie Lou Hamer's testimony was key to the advancement of the modern civil rights movement. Hamer, a sharecropper from Mississippi, was a crusader who faced powerful white male leaders to reveal the abuse and torture that Black people faced for attempting to vote in the United States. In August 1964, Hamer delivered a message to the Democratic National Convention. Her testimony and organizing challenged the white supremacist political power structure of the South and of the entire Democratic Party. Her words had a lasting impact upon the democratic process in her home state: in the following years, Blacks in Mississippi increasingly participated in politics and secured seats and offices that represented the concerns of their communities. While Hamer's own foray into political office was unsuccessful, she was a powerful activist who worked to secure not only voting rights but proper assistance for the poor, children, and the elderly in the Mississippi Delta.

Fifty-four years after Hamer's testimony, Pamela Sue Rush of Lowndes County, Alabama, testified in a congressional hearing about the crushing poverty in which she lived. Rush recounted in her 2018 testimony that she was being charged more than $100,000 for a dilapidated, infested trailer, with raw sewage in her yard. These environmental issues led to ailments for both Rush and her young daughter. Her testimony in 2018 has helped shed light on the injustices facing poor and low-income people in the United States. The conditions in which Rush lived ultimately took her life in 2020. Her partners in the Poor People's Campaign remember her leadership and continue her work to transform the nation.

How is God calling you to respond to the stories and leadership of poor and marginalized women? May the stories of Mary Magdalene, Fannie Lou Hamer, and Pamela Sue Rush inspire you to hear from the poor and the marginalized and to get involved with campaigns against injustice and poverty. May you come to embrace this vision.

— REFLECT —

Are you willing to share your story? Are you willing to respond after listening to the stories of poor and marginalized women in particular, and poor and marginalized people in general?

— READ —

Luke 8. Again here, Jesus responds to women, the poor, and the oppressed.

— PRAY —

God, help us to hear and to believe the stories of women, all people of color, the LGBTQIA2S+ community, immigrants, and others. Give us the wisdom of Magdalene to see the truth, even when others don't believe us. Give us the strength of Fannie Lou Hamer to share our own stories, even in the face of reprisal. And give us the clarity of Pamela Rush to know God wants us to flourish even when the powers of this world tell us the opposite. Amen.

28

TOUCHING THE WOUNDS OF A DISABLED GOD

Letiah Fraser

"Nothing about us without us."

—DISABILITY RIGHTS MOVEMENT SLOGAN,
QUOTED BY ACTIVIST JAMES CHARLTON

READ: JOHN 20:19-31

People with disabilities in Jesus's community were often described by others as "unclean." Today, people with disabilities are often told that we are a liability, a preexisting condition, a burden on the system. We are labeled by our diagnoses. Often disregarded in the hospital room, school, place of employment, religious community, and sometimes even in the home is the *personhood* of those who live with disabilities.

The gospel of John begins by letting us know that the Word became flesh. Jesus became human. The Word had a body. In John 20:19–31, the resurrected Jesus visits the disciples. Thomas is not with them when Jesus visits, however, and has trouble believing the disciples' account. He asks to see the wounds of Jesus, and he continues to be known as the doubting disciple to this day. A week later, all the disciples, including Thomas, are locked in a room because they fear for their lives. (Sounds to me like they all had doubts!) Jesus then appears in the room, bearing the wounds of poverty and the violence of empire. He bears the wounds of a death by state-sanctioned murder.

Today, people with disabilities suffer when state legislatures refuse to pass Medicaid expansion, which disproportionately impacts quality of life. People with disabilities are murdered when insurance companies won't insure those with preexisting conditions or cover medications and treatments that sustain life, and when they refuse to cover durable medical equipment that helps people with disabilities to live independently. In this way, people with disabilities often bear the wounds of poverty and the for-profit health care system.

Thomas has journeyed with Jesus during his three years of earthly ministry; he has a deep faith. Yet he needs an encounter of his own with Jesus. His faith will not be stirred into action solely based on the experience or interpretations of others. I think Thomas both believes the disciples' story *and* believes in fact-checking.

Writer Jon Meacham affirms the practice of investigating your faith for yourself. He writes, "An unexamined faith is not worth having, for fundamentalism and uncritical certitude entail the rejection of one of the great human gifts: that of free will, of the liberty to make up our own minds based on evidence and tradition and reason."

So Thomas asks for what he needs. "Unless I see the nail marks in his hands and put my finger where the nails were, and put my hand into his side, I will not believe." That is a statement of bold faith to me.

Jesus reciprocates Thomas's vulnerability by inviting him not only to see but to touch his disabled body. God in the flesh, in Jesus's resurrected body, is a disabled God.

This disabled God is consonant with the image of Jesus Christ: the stigmatized Jew, the person of color, the representative of the poor and hungry. This disabled God identifies with those who have struggled to maintain the integrity and dignity of their bodies in the face of the physical mutilation of injustice and rituals of bodily degradation.

Jesus's resurrected body is disabled, and through it the personhood and sacredness of each disabled body is made known. It is Thomas's encounter with the disabled God that empowers him to proclaim, "My Lord and my God!"

Ensuring that the bodies and lives of people with disabilities are cared for enables us to see God in one another. As followers of the wounded Christ, we proclaim the personhood and sacredness of each body.

— REFLECT —

What message does this passage reveal about the importance of our bodies? What does it reveal about care for the bodies of those with and without disabilities? How are you caring for your own body and the bodies of others? How does understanding the resurrected Jesus as disabled change your understanding of salvation and resurrection?

— READ —

John 1:9–14. God takes on bodily form in Jesus, as in you.

— PRAY —

Disabled God, there are thirty-two million people who lack health insurance, many of whom have disabilities. Sustain their bodies and minds. Give wisdom to the doctors, compassion to the caregivers, and true justice for us all. Help us honor the personhood and sacredness of each body. Amen.

29

FIND A MULE, SPREAD A MOVEMENT

Clinton Wright

> "There yet remains an energy, when supported with the will that can roll back the combined and encroaching powers of tyranny and injustice."
>
> —FREDERICK DOUGLASS

READ: MATTHEW 21:1-11

A few years ago I was sent to Alabama with the Poor People's Campaign to prepare for our presence in the annual Selma Bridge Crossing Jubilee, a march commemorating Bloody Sunday in 1965. For two weeks I worked throughout town, heralding the good news of the contemporary Poor People's Campaign.

One day I got a call. The voice on the other end said, "We need a mule to pull a wagon for the march."

I was quiet for a moment. "You mean like the mule train that traveled from Mississippi to Washington, D.C., in the 1968 Poor People's Campaign?" Yes, came the reply.

What the . . . ? A mule? How was I going to get a *mule*?

I looked everywhere. I went to farms outside the city. I went to the feed store and asked whether anyone knew where to get a mule. I chased lead after lead after lead. All the while, I was talking to person after person after person about the Poor People's Campaign. I confess I even had thoughts of stealing a mule—but I couldn't find a mule to steal.

We never found one. In the end, we decided to go with a truck and wagon to pull us in that march. Accompanied by hundreds of people from Selma, we demanded that the richest society ever to exist put the needs of the poor first. Ultimately, it wasn't about a mule; it was about building relationships. It wasn't about re-creating the drama of the 1968 campaign; it was about the drama of the right here and right now. An economic system was crushing poor people when it should have been lifting them up from the bottom. That march was about the agency of poor people indicting the system that makes us poor.

Every year on Palm Sunday, we retell the story of Jesus's moral march into Jerusalem, calling to mind the details of this protest. In the shouts of "Hosanna!" we keep in our mind's eye the image of Jesus on a donkey—and it's not just any donkey, but a donkey with her colt, never ridden.

Every time I heard this passage in the past, I would wonder what those disciples said to the owner of the donkey when they got to Bethphage. I hardly think they walked up and said, "Yo! Jesus needs this donkey; we'll be right back," and just ran off with it. It's possible they just stole the donkey and her colt. But from what I know of organizing, I think they likely won the donkey's owner to the movement.

I imagine that the disciples talked about how Rome, the wealthiest economy ever to exist, still took the food the donkey owner needed to feed their family. They might have pointed out that the ruling elites of Judea sat in the temple and the palaces of Jerusalem and cast judgment on the poor, the sick, the orphaned, the widowed. They might have said the army of the Roman Empire was about to march into the city and they needed this donkey to show another way was possible. Luckily for this protest we now call Palm Sunday, somehow they got the donkey and colt.

In the end, this story is not about the donkey or the colt. They are just elements of public and political theater—part of a performance that allows all poor people in Jerusalem to be protagonists in their own liberation. In this grand drama, God is going to ask each of us to do strange things: find a mule, march down a street, go to jail. We must take on these tasks and organize while we do.

And God will sometimes force us to laugh. A few weeks after my failed search for a mule, I landed in Havana, Cuba, to visit with friends and family. As I walked out of the airport, I saw a man riding in a wagon pulled by a mule. I had finally found my mule!

God is always with the poor and oppressed. God will always challenge us to make a way out of no way. When we organize to take back what is rightfully ours, God will always be by our side.

— REFLECT —

What drama is playing out in your community? Is the drama controlled by those in power or by the powerful people organizing for justice around you? What is your role in this drama?

— READ —

Psalm 118. In the remaining verses of Matthew 21, Jesus quotes Psalm 118:22: "The stone the builders rejected has become the cornerstone." As movement people of faith, we must begin to see this protest march as a groundbreaking ceremony, a cornerstone-laying event.

— PRAY —

God, we thank you for the strange things you ask us to do. May we continue to heed your call to take back what is ours. As the stones refused by the rulers of our society, we ask you to guide us to lay our bodies on the line. Make us cornerstones of your justice. Amen.

PART IV
LEARN AS WE LEAD

30

IS IT REALLY ALL THAT BAD?

Aaron Scott

"Homelessness is growing, the so-called middle class is disappearing-the problems have gotten worse. People only see the US through TV sets, and hear what the main representatives of the US government have to say about it. But there are two countries, and one of them-the one I am part of-is not heard from. But this is the one that is going to be heard because the people are not going to sit back for much longer and allow their families and kids to starve and allow the conditions to continue to deteriorate, threatening their lives. History has proved this and I think that we got to get ready for those times. We got to dig deep among the people who are hurting, the real masses in this country, so that we can give organization and unity to a movement that can really better the conditions here. There is no reason why we should have homelessness and poverty in this country or in the world because we have the capacity to produce enough for everybody."

—WILLIE BAPTIST

READ: AMOS 8:1-12

We often think prophets sound far-fetched. Their words are so strong, their condemnations so scathing. We ask, "Is it *really* all that bad?" But prophets are here to pull our heads out of the sand. They make us face the truths in our society and in our history that, unless we change, will be our collective undoing. Prophets are here to remind us that being well adjusted in a sick society is the deepest sickness of all.

What did the prophet Amos see at the temple, in the places of power, in the slums? What casual acts of brutality against the weak did he witness on the street corners? Which merchants did he see in the market, prioritizing a few coins over a hungry family's survival?

Amos saw in his time that the present reality of the poor would be the future reality of his whole society. Famine, mourning, exploitation, death, endless wandering without rest or safety, all the flavors of doom that Amos said were coming upon his nation: these realities had already come for the poor. Amos lived in a deeply unequal society, where some people were doing quite well for themselves and many others were living in misery. He saw that this economic system, which was the material manifestation of a moral system, would eventually be its own undoing.

Today we are seeing the same thing, in this stage of crisis in our own nation.

If we want to go where Amos is trying to lead us, toward redemption and freedom, we have to do two things. First: we must understand that as long as we allow poverty to exist at all, our entire society is vulnerable. Poor people are not the problem. A society that allows poverty to exist is the problem. Second: we must recognize the authority of poor people. We must hear the voices of the poor not only out of sympathy but with the soul-deep awareness that any one of us who isn't poor right now could be next. As long as we allow poverty to exist, we will all be plagued by the spiritual and material sickness of the world.

We name Amos as our prophet, and it's his words that made it into our Scripture. Yet it was actually the words and cries and lives and deaths of the poor of his time that prophesied to Amos himself. Amos walked among the poor and listened to their bone-deep pain. He learned that, yes, it really *was* that bad.

Through their cries, the poor showed him what would inevitably come to pass for his whole society. Today we are being shown the same. The prophets are desperately calling toward us, demanding that we listen.

— REFLECT —

Can you think of a time you witnessed people in power betraying the well-being of poor folks just to make a dollar? What thoughts and feelings came up for you in that moment? What words would you speak to name the inequities in your community?

— READ —

Mark 10:41–48. In this passage, Jesus offers his perspective on power, how it truly looks and acts.

— PRAY —

Creator, you give each of us the insight and ability of the prophets. Help us remember: we don't need fancy degrees or five-dollar words to tell the truth. We just need to hear you, trust you, and speak! Amen.

31

BLAME THE POOR OR JUDGE THE RICH?

Liz Theoharis

> "Christianity is being concerned about [others], not building a million-dollar church while people are starving right around the corner. Christ was a revolutionary person, out there where it was happening."
>
> **—FANNIE LOU HAMER**

READ: 2 THESSALONIANS 3

"He who does not work shall not eat." The first time I heard this text (2 Thessalonians 3:10 TLB) was as a welfare rights activist in Philadelphia in the 1990s. In the lead-up to the 1996 welfare reform act, politicians, religious leaders, and others quoted this verse to justify shutting down food programs and kicking mothers and their babies off public assistance.

I grew up well versed in the Bible. But it was not until these leaders, many of them Christian, warped the biblical message of abundance for all and weaponized this verse (and others) to justify blaming the poor for poverty that I dove further into interpreting texts. I began to see the parallels between the moral and political agency of poor and homeless people of the welfare rights movement and the early Christians, who set up mutual aid societies and burial associations of the poor. Although forced to live without adequate housing, food, education, or health care, they protested injustice at the beginning of the first millennium. As I explored the development of the early Christian movement, I saw that both back then and today, leaders figure out how to meet each other's needs.

I delved into deeper biblical study and learned about a battle for the Bible throughout history. How slaveholders produced a Bible that excluded the exodus, the prophets, and Jesus's inaugural sermon about preaching good news to the poor and release to the captives. I read how abolitionists like Frederick Douglass and Harriet Tubman called forth a freedom church tradition and referenced biblical teachings that included proclaiming liberty throughout the land. I learned about social gospel proponents preaching responsibility and bounty and abundance for all on earth.

A battle for the Bible continues today, especially when it comes to the passage from Paul's second letter to the Thessalonians about working and eating. In debates about social welfare programs in the twenty-first century, a Texas representative quoted 2 Thessalonians to justify increasing work requirements for people qualifying for Supplemental Nutrition Assistance Program (SNAP), a low-income food assistance program. He rebuffed a representative of the Jewish antihunger group MAZON who referenced Leviticus to speak to the commandment to feed the hungry. Other representatives used 2 Thessalonians to justify cutting food stamps.

But despite its manipulation by those in power, this verse from 2 Thessalonians 3 is not blaming the poor for their poverty and misery. Indeed, it is judging the rich.

The dynamics taking place in the early Christian communities are taken up in 2 Thessalonians. The letter implores those who inherited resources—those who have so much wealth that they do not have to work to survive—to see building a world where everyone has enough as their responsibility. These lazy, wealthier people—those who are disrupting the early Christian community—are expected to work and not just benefit from the toil of low-wage workers and the poor.

The most serious problem for the residents of the urban centers of the empire, including those who received the letters to the Thessalonians, was securing enough food and sustenance. Starvation was prevalent. The poor were wanting in clothes, housing, health care, and any form of an adequate standard of living. They suffered from injuries at work and regular violence. Old age was not common because of these harsh conditions of life. Indeed, starvation was the historical context of 2 Thessalonians. Yet a number of wealthier people—some playing roles in maintaining the Roman imperial structures and others with inherited wealth and largesse—were also a part of the emerging Christian community.

So when the author of 2 Thessalonians 3 critiques those who are not working but benefiting from the work of others, it is not an instruction against caring for the poor. It is a judgment against the rich for the ways they are exploiting God's chosen people and they must stop.

— REFLECT —

Where have you heard a message of blame and judgment of the poor when the rich and powerful are the ones to be judged? How does the existence of poverty and inequality in our communities take away from God's grace and promise of abundance?

— READ —

James 5. "The wages you failed to pay the workers who mowed your fields are crying out against you. The cries of the harvesters have reached the ears of the Lord Almighty" (5:4). Like 2 Thessalonians, this passage names and places clear blame on the moral failures of those in power.

— PRAY —

God of those who hunger and thirst for justice and those who work hard—often in multiple poverty-wage jobs—but who still cannot afford adequate food, we pray that you spread your spirit on those crying out for justice and abundance. Everybody's got a right to live: this indeed is your will. Amen.

32

PERSISTENCE OF THE POOR

Erica N. Williams

> "Sometimes it seems like to tell the truth today is to run the risk of being killed. But if I fall, I'll fall five feet four inches forward in the fight for freedom. I'm not backing off."
>
> **—FANNIE LOU HAMER**

READ: LUKE 18

The people of Flint, Michigan, were given poison to drink so the city could pay its bills. Before the now well-known water crisis took place, the state of Michigan had employed an emergency manager to oversee the city after an audit projected a $25 million deficit. In an effort to save money, the emergency manager, supervised by the governor, decided to switch the water supply from the Detroit River to the Flint River. The water in the Flint River was so bad that the General Motors plant had stopped using it; the high levels of chlorine were eroding engine parts. At the time, Flint had the highest poverty rate among cities in Michigan over sixty-five thousand people. In a city that once thrived due to the automotive industry, about 40 percent of people were living at or below the poverty line.

Essentially, the residents of Flint had their democracy stolen. The state government told them, "Because you are poor and we can no longer exploit your labor, we are going to give you water laced with lead." Testing revealed the water had 104 parts per billion (ppb) of lead, nearly seven times greater than the Environmental Protection Agency limit of 15 parts per billion. The Flint water crisis devastated the lives of the people of Flint, and the government did everything in its power to cover up what happened. President Barack Obama even went to Flint to drink a glass of water to say that the water was safe to drink—all while the contaminated pipes had yet to be fixed.

In the midst of all the lies and corruption, a grassroots group of people in Flint, just like the persistent widow in the passage of Luke 18:1–8, would not allow the authorities to deny them justice. In the Bible, the persistent widow keeps going to the judge and demanding justice. He won't give her the time of day—until he realizes that she is going to beat him down if she does not get what she wants. The judge thinks he can ignore this woman, who is poor and considered an outcast. But she knows she is powerful, and she is going to persist until the judge realizes it too. The widow could be harmed and even killed because of her protesting, but that does not stop her; she keeps her eyes on the prize.

This story reminds me of Claire McClinton, a longtime activist and organizer in Flint who helped to lead the fight against the government in the water crisis. I will never forget being at a Water Warriors conference in Detroit and hearing Claire explain how pregnant mothers were losing their babies, people were facing chronic health challenges, and the children of Flint would be impacted for generations to come. Claire cried as she talked about how the people in Flint were getting the runaround from public officials, and how the state was working hard to silence the voices of those fighting back. Through her tears, Claire decreed that the people were not going to lie down and die. She declared boldly that she planned to fight until justice was served, and she has done just that.

Years later, the water crisis is still not over. But some relief and vindication have come, thanks to the work of Claire and many others. The state of Michigan was forced to pay $600 million to the victims of Flint. Even though no amount of money can repair the damage this crisis caused, we take note of the persistence of the poor and dispossessed people in Flint, who will not be denied the justice they deserve.

I see the persistent widow embodied in the lives of Poor People's Campaign leader Callie Greer, who lost her daughter Venus because she didn't have health care. Callie continues to fight for the right to health care for all. I see her in Mashyla Buckmaster, a young mom who was forced to live on the streets but is organizing with Chaplains by the Harbor, and in Wendsler Nosie, the leader of Apache Stronghold who has given his life to fighting to keep multinational copper mining companies from destroying the most sacred sites of the Apache people, and in Kenia Torres-Alcocer, an undocumented mom and organizer.

All over the nation—Including in Flint, Michigan as well as Selma, Alabama, Westport, Washington, San Carlos, Arizona, and Los Angeles, California—the poor and rejected are rising up and declaring to the nation that all power belongs to the people. If we don't get no justice, you will not get any peace.

— REFLECT —

Where do you see the persistence of the poor? Name the people who embody the persistent widow for you. What is the justice they demand? How can you add your voice?

— READ —

Genesis 21:14-21. The powerful story of Hagar shows us that God hears and responds to cries for justice.

— PRAY —

Creator, grant us the spirit of the persistent widow and all those who, when their backs are against the wall, persist for justice in spite of their plight. Ashe and amen.

33

IN THE BEGINNING, THERE WAS CARE

Solita Alexander Riley

"We have an uneven appreciation of everybody's sacred worth. There is an importance of reconnecting with our original spirituality. When you separate people from the land, you alienate people from their ability to experience their connection. In the process, it starts waves of disconnection from the people who are around them, to the people who are no longer next to them, and it becomes easy to label people as 'other' and not worthy. If we are going to be well spiritually, then we have to re-embrace what we had in the very beginning and that is our recognition of the spirituality of everything and everyone. There is something of value in everything. We are all worthy. We are all related."

—TRINI RODRIGUEZ

READ: GENESIS 1, 2

In the beginning, who was there? Not you, not me. How then can we account for that time? We can easily tell each other stories of what happened yesterday, and history books offer stories of the recent past. But eons ago, when nothing yet existed? Who knows that story?

Creation stories abound, in all cultures and faiths. Like any tale passed down orally or otherwise, origin stories are subject to the storyteller's perspective. The person telling the story gets to give *their* version. That's true for the creation stories we find in the Bible, in Genesis 1 and 2. In this particular attempt to explain the mystery of humankind, all living things, and the earth itself, we find two different versions of the same story.

These creation stories have been broadcast and translated over thousands of years, by various groups hoping to legitimize authority and power. Yet these Genesis stories carry truths that we need to examine and apply. In them, we see the truth of our own inherent potential. We see a system of life that revolves around providing care—a universe that literally rests on care. And we see that we need partnership to keep creation, keep care, going.

Genesis 1 and 2 show that there is potential—there is more—within each aspect of creation. God establishes the heavens, the lights, and the waters and then pulls life from the earth, the seas, and the land. God doesn't put fish into the oceans; the water brings them forth, as the land brings forth various animals. So something within the water and land could be brought out. And as God tells the various animals, including the human, to be fruitful and multiply, there is further suggestion of the great capacity—the great power for more—inherent within each.

Many of us who are poor now bear the daily assaults of an oppressive system—one that has seemingly forgotten our value, our power, and our ability to contribute and create. Yet we can be sure we each have these things, and we can know God is calling them all forward. God is calling us to continue to live and create yet more life.

What should this life look like? And how and what should we be creating? At the very least, it ought to look like caring.

When we read Genesis 1 and 2 and beyond, we see that God provides for needs in abundance. Each type of animal, including humans, is given food to eat from some part of the established creation. The aspects of creation are not operating in isolation from or competition with each other; they are resting in relationship with each other. Sustenance is found and life is sustained when we are in right relationship with all aspects of creation. We do not live in a bubble. The quality of each life depends on another.

Then we read that God creates human partnership. In short, God creates a system whereby all material and emotional life is tended to. So if we are to be fruitful and multiply—if we are to add to creation—the systems we create must extend the provision of care.

Unfortunately, our systems of care in the United States need serious attention. So many people go without adequate medical care because of high bills and the tenuous nature of Medicaid and health care. Families have difficulty securing food, housing, and clean water. The system stresses personal responsibility more than the need for public assistance or the consequences of corporate irresponsibility. In these ways and more, they fly in the face of the system of care that God set in motion in the beginning. These are not fruitful systems. They do not multiply, add to, or sustain life; they end it. So they must be re-created.

Within each of us lies the potential to create and re-create a system that revolves around and produces care, a system where needs are met. We will need each other to do so. We will need to be in partnership, working together to be fruitful and multiply. We will need to be in right relationship with each other, and all creation, to add to what God has started and to create life-sustaining systems of care, as God commands us.

The beginning of the story has been written, told, and retold, and the end of the story will be the sum of our choices. So let the living of our lives reflect the potential, the partnership, and the caring as it was in the beginning, that life may be everlasting.

— REFLECT —

How is God taking care of you? What are your needs? Which systems—which aspects of human creation—care for you? Which put your life at risk? Where is there potential for change? Who is or can be your partner in creating life-sustaining change?

— READ —

Matthew 6:26–34. This passage helps us remember that our needs become satisfied in pursuing God's rule of care.

— PRAY —

Oh God, thank you for all your creation. Thank you for providing all I need, for considering me worthy to live. Thank you for your care and for empowering us to create systems that continue the care you began. Forgive us where we fail. Please open our eyes that we may see how to be fruitful and multiply, to partner in the ways of life everlasting. Amen.

34

A HURT AND ANGRY GOD

Daniel Jones

"Every day we're not organizing the working class, as a class, united across lines of division, is a day we're losing ground."

—NIJMIE DZURINKO

READ: HOSEA 8:1-14, 10:12-13

Hosea says to the rulers of ancient Israel that they have rejected God. In their greed, in their love of buying and selling, in their oppression of the poor, in their immoral religious nationalism, and in their pursuit of military alliances and military strength: in these things, they have made a choice. God, in turn, has rejected both them and the society they have reshaped in their own graven image and in servitude to themselves.

These *mis*leaders, says Hosea, are sowing the wind of injustice. And they will reap the whirlwind of a crisis of violence and hunger and death that even they won't be able to escape.

More than 2,500 years later, we know that Hosea was right. The kings and officers and priests of Israel fell. None of their self-sanctifying ritual, focus on economic growth and trade, or military and diplomatic bargaining could save them from the consequences of having subverted justice, manipulated the courts against the poor, and pursued policies of exploitation, foreclosure, and eviction.

Hosea is not a particularly hopeful prophet. There was little to be hopeful for, especially in the short term. Hosea is the prophet of a hurt and angry God, whose people have been kept from God's teachings and blessings by illegitimate and immoral rulers.

But in the midst of this pain and anger, he strikes a rare note of hope and possibility for renewal. He tells us that while kings and their priests sow wickedness, we are called to sow righteousness and that this too will bear fruit. He tells us we can break new ground and till new soil and plant new seeds right now. When we read this, we have to ask ourselves: What does it mean to sow the kind of righteousness that will allow our own society, in its time of violent crisis that so resembles Hosea's, to choose a new path?

We can take this idea of sowing and planting seriously. It speaks to us of long-term thinking. These crises in our society are going to get deeper as long as our own rulers and officers and their high priests (religious and secular) remain in power. The crises are beyond their control. As they double down on their faithless and immoral policies, seeking help from places that cannot provide it, they will only make it worse.

Sowing righteousness—creating the possibility for righteousness to become the law of the land—is what we are called to do. Who holds the power to make our nation turn away from the path of destruction? It's the poor, the organized, and the united. Sowing righteousness means creating the conditions for the poor to take action together in the face of determined opposition. We're sowing righteousness when we break new ground, organizing in the places that are often skipped over and among the people who are often written off—even though mistakes abound and victories can be rare and precious. We're sowing righteousness when we devote ourselves to the growth and the flourishing of other leaders—even though mentorship is demanding and education is a difficult art.

Whether we win or lose in the short term, we struggle against the wickedness of immoral policies. We sow righteousness as we plant seeds of organization and leadership and nourish them for times of even greater possibility.

— REFLECT —

How am I called to sow righteousness today? Who do I see around me sowing righteousness and breaking new ground for new possibility?

— READ —

Matthew 13:1–23. Jesus addresses our role as sower and helps us each consider our condition as soil.

— PRAY —

Source of righteousness, every day you create the possibility of new beginnings. We seek your presence sincerely, and we open ourselves to your judgment. Help us to break up new ground and plant the seeds of goodness today that we may enjoy justice in times to come. Amen.

35

STEADFAST SPIRIT FOR JUSTICE

Claire Chadwick

> "One night, a juror came to Jesus and he wanted
> to know what he could do to be saved. . . . Instead
> of getting bogged down on one thing, Jesus looked
> at him and said, 'Nicodemus, you must be born
> again.' . . . In other words, 'Your whole structure must
> be changed.'"
>
> —MARTIN LUTHER KING JR.

READ: PSALM 51:1-12

Throughout history, the phrases of this psalm—"Have mercy on me, O God" and "Create in me a pure heart"—have often been read as words of penitence. They have been reworked and added to music, sung as a tune begging for forgiveness after an individual transgression. And, indeed, they read easily that way: as though the writer has committed a sin and is seeking repentance and forgiveness for that individual act. This psalm has traditionally been associated with David, probably because in the Hebrew Bible we read about the many sins that David has committed.

But what if this particular passage—and the psalms of lament in general—aren't just talking about personal sins? What if we read the psalmist as lamenting something far more wicked: the sins of a society that turns its back on the poor?

In Kansas, among grassroots leaders building a movement to end poverty, this is where we begin in our distinct understanding of sin. Today, Kansas is one of a dozen states that has not expanded Medicaid, which leaves a coverage gap for people who earn "too much" money to be able to access Medicaid but far too little to purchase quality health insurance. In 2020, that accounted for about 150,000 Kansans who made poverty-level wages. And although the majority of Kansans want to expand Medicaid—it's the bare minimum the state could do to guarantee health care access to its citizens—the legislation was stopped in committee by a few extremist senators.

During organizing meetings in our fight for health care, we had intense discussions about how best to address this legislative stunt. We discussed why so many people being denied health care did not believe they had the power to exact it. We began to understand both the action of halting the legislation *and* the inaction of so many Kansans who said they wanted Medicaid but did not show up to demand it as transgressions.

We determined that the sin of denying health care coverage to those who receive poverty wages needed a public indictment. We needed to inspire Kansans to believe that it didn't have to be this way. We had to make it clear that by denying health care access to 150,000 Kansans, these legislators were signing the death certificates of the poor and low-income folks who fell into the coverage gap. Inaction left blood on their hands. The banners that we dropped inside the State House from the balcony floor stated just that. Inscribed with the names of these particular legislators, the banners said, "Blood On Their Hands." It was vital to us that Kansans understood that this legislative inaction, rooted in greed and the desire for power, was causing death.

What if this psalm is not just about David's personal transgressions but about those of a nation? Transgressions, after all, aren't just about wrongdoing but are about a lack of justice. Our elected leaders sin when they deny health care access in order to hold on to political power. This is transgression. And just as it states in the psalm: your sin is ever before you.

What we, as freedom fighters, can take from the psalm comes to us in verse 10: "Create in me a pure heart, O God, and renew a steadfast spirit within me." We must remain steadfast in the fight. Despite the continued sins of those in power, we must fight on, just a little while longer.

"Your whole structure must be changed," Rev. Dr. King told us, in explaining how our society must be redeemed. It will take a movement of the people to do so.

— REFLECT —

What are some sins or transgressions in your community that are about social injustice and social sin? How are people challenging the sins of racism and poverty?

— READ —

John 3:1–21. As Jesus talks with Nicodemus in this passage, we are invited to examine God's desire for our individual reorientation and collective restructuring. This passage centers love as God's motivation.

— PRAY —

God of justice, please help all your children to hold on just a little while longer. Give your people the strength and the knowledge to proclaim, "I know justice is coming soon." Amen.

36

EXPOSE YOURSELF, EXPOSE THE EMPIRE

Adam Barnes

"This is a Third Reconstruction moment, just like after slavery and after the Brown decision. It's a time to restructure and reorder all of society. When racists killed Emmett Till, Rosa Parks decided to take down Jim Crow. When Jimmie Lee Jackson was killed, Amelia Boynton and others took down voter suppression. We need to change the system and the people running the system."

—WILLIAM J. BARBER II

READ: MATTHEW 5:38-42

In May 2020, a police officer in Minneapolis murdered George Floyd by kneeling on his neck for nearly nine minutes. This particularly brutal and highly visible act of police violence ignited a wave of outrage and protest across the country. An estimated fifteen million to twenty-five million people hit the streets in more than three thousand cities and towns; half of them said it was their first protest.

Like other moments in history, this particular incident existed in a long line of oppression and galvanized a movement. We were outraged at the continued dehumanization of Black bodies, and we were fed up with a social system that uses the military and police to enforce laws and policies that hurt the poor and protect the position of elites. In the courageous tradition of Emmett Till's mother, who insisted on an open-casket funeral after her son's murder, and of Rosa Parks, who took on segregation by placing her body at the front of a bus, countless new leaders moved into the movement.

Two thousand years ago, Jesus awakened people to the reality facing them as they lived under the Roman Empire: either the poor get organized and confront this system or it will continue to kill us. The same choice faces us today. This system is killing us—whether immediately and brutally, as through police violence, or slowly, as through poverty-related causes that studies suggest mean death to at least 250,000 people in the United States each year.

How can the poor and dispossessed realistically confront and defeat such an overwhelming force? Longtime movement leader Willie Baptist offers this advice: "We can't out-spend them; we can't out-might them; but we can out-smart them." In Matthew 5:38–42, Jesus offers tactics to help the poor get smart and organized. He also offers deep spiritual resources for how to reclaim dignity and live into an alternative vision of the world: the kingdom of God, not the kingdom of Caesar.

Jesus begins by recalling a well-known instruction on justice from Hebrew Scripture: "You have heard that it was said, 'Eye for eye, and tooth for tooth'" (5:38; see also Exodus 21:24 and Leviticus 24:19–21). Seemingly in contrast to this lesson, Jesus instructs his audience in a new way, instructing them "not to resist an evil person" and to "turn the other cheek." Christians have often used this passage to say we should be meek and nonconfrontational. Good Christians, the argument goes, should submit to established forms of power and, in exchange, receive eternal life after death.

But this is not what Jesus is teaching. If we take a closer look at just one part, the instruction to hand over your cloak if someone sues you for it, we see a profound lesson about sources of power for poor people—namely, nonviolent resistance.

Jesus portrays an experience the poor would be familiar with: being so poor that the only way to cover one's debt is to give away one's shirt. If this happens, give away your cloak as well, says Jesus. According to biblical scholar Walter Wink, this would have left the person completely—and publicly—naked. In Jewish tradition, more shame would fall on the person who made another person naked than on the one whose nakedness is exposed. Jesus's instruction therefore robs the oppressor, in this case the creditor, of their power to humiliate. It puts on public display the cruelty of the powerful and unjust system they uphold.

Systems of oppression, in the Roman Empire and today, create false moral narratives to justify violence of all kinds against the poor. Jesus teaches us how to subvert these systems and expose their domination. Like the original Jesus movement, movements today must go up against forces that have a virtual monopoly over military and police power. To win, we must "out-smart" our opponent.

The legacy of these tactics today is nonviolent civil disobedience, which exposes systemic injustice. Creative public actions dare the system to show itself for what it really is. Reading Matthew from this perspective helps reclaim Jesus as a revolutionary leader of the poor. It helps us consider our tactics today and reimagine them not simply as clever ways to get small concessions but as glimpses of a coming revolution. As Walter Wink says in *Engaging the Powers*, "There is no reason to wait until Rome has been defeated. . . . The reign of God is already breaking into the world."

— REFLECT —

Why is it important that tactics of nonviolent direct action be part of a larger strategy and moral vision? How have these tactics been neutralized in our current context? How can we reimagine them to respond to what we are up against today?

— READ —

Luke 17:20–37. As the routines and functions of daily life are carried out, the rule of God breaks forth in undeniable fashion, destroying that which is already broken and dead.

— PRAY —

God of the poor and brokenhearted, you have shown us how violence is overcome by loving and caring for life, not by violating and degrading it. Help us find the courage and creativity to resist and to love. Amen.

37

BEASTLY ECONOMICS

C. Wess Daniels

> "Revelation's notion of ultimate evil is best understood today as systemic evil and structural sin."
>
> **—ELISABETH SCHÜSSLER FIORENZA**

READ: REVELATION 13

The "mark of the beast" and the number 666 run through popular American culture. Some use them in deadly serious terms—as prophecy marking nonbelievers, liberals, and those seen as standing against "Christian values." Others make jokes about end-times weirdos who rant about birthmarks and barcodes. But both miss Revelation's point.

Revelation isn't a letter predicting the end of the world or instructions for how to evacuate earth. Nor is it a fantasy to be dismissed or mocked. Rather, it is a handbook for how the early church, made up of marginalized people, could resist and survive the Roman Empire.

The mark of the beast is not a symbol found on the forehead of an evil person that we can identify and ostracize. It's much worse than that. To the first readers of Revelation, it is both a symbol and an ongoing pattern of an evil and oppressive system that consumes all. The mark of the beast is how Revelation describes the oppressive economic system of the Roman Empire, not a mark that identifies unbelievers. Revelation unmasks the economics of empire by rooting it in the image of the beast—an image that runs counter to being made in the "image of God" (Genesis 1).

The Roman Empire marked its subjects. Wes Howard-Brook and Anthony Gwyther write in *Unveiling Empire* that the *charagma* ("mark") was the "official seal for business contracts." The mark was "branding impressed upon prisoners and slaves. And upon religious devotees of the Imperial religion." Importantly, the empire's coinage, the *denarius*, was also marked with the image of Caesar, who was considered to be the son of god in the Roman imperial religion.

The economic system of empire is not just something you participate in; like a devotee of a religion, you have to believe in it. Any questioning—any challenging of the prevailing economic system—and you are seen as a heretic, or worse ("all who refused to worship the image," Revelation 13:15 says, might be killed).

Have you ever challenged the underpinnings of capitalism? Called into question why some people are "worth" getting paid $350,000 a year while others struggle to live on $35,000 or much less? Have your questions been treated kindly or as heretical? Beastly economics is based on immoral theology about the wealthy and the poor. It is visible whenever we see who is prioritized and how we prioritize our spending as a country.

The distorted theology of beastly economics—embodied by the bronze sculpture of the bull on Wall Street—convinces many politicians, preachers, and citizens that only when the golden calf is taken care of can the rest of us get what we need. First the billionaires need their tax cuts; then we'll see what is left. It is beastly economics under which Congress (Democratic and Republican members alike) operates when it allows billions of dollars to go to corporations and the military but cuts basic funding for education and health care.

Poverty in this country is the result of the beastly economics of empire. It is what the first readers of Revelation faced and what so many of the great traditions of resistance have struggled against throughout history.

The system is not broken; this is how it is meant to work. The rich continue to fill their pockets and game the system, while millions of people who struggle to survive on poverty wages are called lazy. This is the empire that God calls us to resist.

When the preachers of empire defang Revelation of its real prophetic critique, they can continue benefiting from the mark that accompanies the religion of empire. When others neuter this book so that it is no longer a tool for helping us to resist empire, everybody loses.

Instead of getting caught up in reaction to the empire, we can be enveloped and formed by the Lamb that was slain—the Lamb who is alive, and who shapes an alternative community in the midst of empire.

— REFLECT —

Where has beastly economics done the most damage in your community? How is God calling you and your community to resist it? How is God calling you to support prophetic witness against harmful economic systems?

— READ —

Deuteronomy 17. This passage helps us understand the nature of true sacrifice and worship.

— PRAY —

Jesus, help us to understand rightly the pressing economic issues of our time. Help us be clear-sighted in our support of just economic practices and reject those that exploit your creation for personal gain. Amen.

38

LEARN AS WE LEAD

Jessica C. Williams

> "I have always thought that what is needed is the development of people who are interested not in being leaders as much as in developing leadership in others."
>
> —ELLA BAKER

READ: ACTS 6-7

The life of Stephen, a Greek-speaking follower of Jesus, is a chapter in the story of the early movement of believers. These Jesus followers were living together in community and trying to meet each other's basic needs in the midst of the oppression of the Roman Empire (see Acts 4). Stephen is often known as the first martyr of the Christian church, but he has so much more to teach us than simply that. His is a story of leadership development and of the leadership of the poor and dispossessed. Through Stephen's story, we learn more about what it means to develop leaders who embody clarity, commitment, connectedness, and competency—what leaders in the Kairos Center and Poor People's Campaign call the four Cs of leadership.

The leadership of the poor and dispossessed is a fundamental principle of the Poor People's Campaign because we believe that the poor and dispossessed can best develop the insight and knowledge to lead the changes needed in our society so that all may live and thrive. In our study of history, including the poor communities in the Bible that organized for liberation, we see that those most affected by injustice can best lead us all toward change. And in our study of the Bible, we can see that God often calls the oppressed, the marginalized, and those least expected to lead God's people to liberation.

Yet we who are poor and dispossessed often don't see ourselves as leaders because we have received false messages from society about what leadership looks like, who leaders are, and where they come from. Too often we internalize these messages and have a hard time believing that we are called by God to develop into leaders who can change society.

The Bible tells us a different story, and Stephen is an example of that. Stephen is identified as someone who could be developed into a leader for his community. He is asked, along with six others, to lead an organizing committee to help meet the needs of the Greek-speaking widows within the early church community. Others around him have seen that he is "full of faith and of the Holy Spirit" (6:5). As is true for many leaders in our movement, someone else sees his leadership qualities before he does. As part of a community, we can develop those gifts and learn how to organize to meet the needs of those in our community. Stephen's election to this role is an example of how leaders within the movement are identified and developed.

The four Cs of leadership—clarity, commitment, connectedness, and competency—are not qualities that we possess at birth. Instead, we learn them through our collective work to build the unity of the poor and dispossessed and change conditions in society. To develop *clarity* and *competency*, we must study history, Scripture, and our current context to understand how to forge ahead for social change. We do that through our *connectedness* with the movement, with other leaders, and with communities. And we develop *commitment* to the work, to one another, and to building the world that God desires; we learn to "stick and stay" through the ups and downs of fighting for justice.

We can see these four Cs of leadership in the story of Stephen's development as a leader. Acts 7 shows that he has studied history, Scripture, and the context of oppression under the Roman Empire. He is connected to his Greek-speaking community and able to lead through a time of tension within the larger community of the early church. And he is so committed to the cause that he is eventually martyred while praying for those who would take his life.

Countless leaders within the Poor People's Campaign have committed their lives to the movement to end poverty, and they are continually developing other leaders to do the same. As you work your way through this devotional book, you are reading the words of many of these leaders. Like Stephen did, we follow in the footsteps of a great many leaders who have called and developed others to carry the baton forward.

Moses, Miriam, Esther, Mary, Jesus, Gandhi, Martin, Ella: we whose names are listed in this book join this great cloud of witnesses as we lead. And we invite you to join us!

— REFLECT —

What are your gifts of leadership? Who has identified and developed you as a leader? How have you influenced the development of other leaders for the movement? Who are the leaders you know who have been shaped for movements of faith and justice?

— READ —

1 Samuel 3, Esther 2, Matthew 4:18-21, and Luke 10:38-42. These Scriptures will help you learn about the calling and development of other leaders in the freedom movements in the Bible.

— PRAY —

Holy God, here I am. Where are you calling me to go? Who are you putting in my path to grow with as leaders? We give thanks for those you have placed in our lives who have helped us to see ourselves as leaders despite what society may tell us. Give us the wisdom to develop more leaders for this movement of freedom and liberation. Amen.

PART V

THE ADVENT OF REVOLUTION

39

WHAT DOTH THE LORD REQUIRE?

Liz Theoharis

"If you are neutral in situations of injustice, you have chosen the side of the oppressor. If an elephant has its foot on the tail of a mouse and you say that you are neutral, the mouse will not appreciate your neutrality."

—DESMOND TUTU

READ: MICAH 6:6-8

My mom died a month before I wrote this chapter. A fierce activist for peace and justice, she dedicated herself my entire life to organizing for the human rights of all people, an end to war and global conflict, interreligious understanding, and the abolition of poverty and racism.

From the age of three, I was going to protests with her in our hometown of Milwaukee. In preschool, I would bring a Winnie the Pooh bag filled with coloring books to church and movement meetings with her. By elementary and middle school, we were taking part in antiracist day camps and citywide protests and concerts together. Throughout high school and college, I got involved in many of the causes my mom championed. And when I joined the movement to end poverty, led by the poor, my mom joined too.

She would often jest that moms know everything. (Beneath the smile, she believed it true.) And when it came to the justice that God requires, my mom sure knew a lot. She knew that in the richest country in the world, we do not have a scarcity of resources but a scarcity of political will. Likewise, she knew that charity cannot undo inequality and that it will take nothing less than a nation organized around the needs of the poor and suffering.

She knew that to work for peace and justice in the United States requires internationalism—that we must care for those in South Africa, in Russia, in Palestine, in El Salvador, in Sudan, in Syria, in Pakistan, in Cleveland and Detroit and Montgomery. Everywhere. Everyone. She knew that freedom fighters throughout the ages have had to organize, and mobilize, and educate, and agitate for freedom, equality, moral healing, and jubilee justice.

My mom's favorite Bible passage—and the password for her computer, phone messages, and online accounts—was always Micah 6:8. She knew that doing justice, loving kindness, and walking humbly with God were the true instructions for living a faithful and impactful life. Her faith and activism were one.

Micah 6:6–8 is a typical story of the prophets. Biblical prophets tell the people what is necessary for honoring and worshipping God. Indeed, they all tell the same story: that God desires mercy, justice, and peace, especially for the poor, the widows, the suffering, and the victims of war. The prophets admonish us and the ruling authorities to work for peace and dedicate ourselves to ending poverty.

The book of Micah instructs that the only way to honor and worship God is to welcome the immigrant neighbor, the homeless, and the bruised and battered. Micah says we must overcome bias and inequality and advocate for all God's children to have what they need to thrive, not merely and barely survive.

Today there are too many injustices, too much hate and violence, and too many religious people proclaiming that the only moral issues of our day are gun rights, property rights, and laws that say who can marry whom. In these days, we can go back to Micah and be reminded of what God requires. We can learn what the Bible really says about justice and about how to organize society around the needs of the people, care for the least of these, practice peace, and allow all to live in abundance and dignity.

God does not ask for luxurious gifts, nor for the sacrifice of lives and livelihoods. God instead wants all people to prosper—for no one to have too much while others have too little. God demands justice, not charity or sacrifice. God longs for the righting of wrongs, the repairing of breaches.

Throughout the book of Micah, the people suffer. In the prophet Micah's time, like now, there is violence in the world. But at the end of Micah 7, there is hope again. Micah 7:7 reads, "But as for me, I watch in hope for the Lord, I wait for God my Savior; my God will hear me."

Justice is possible. I learn this from the prophet Micah. I learn this from my fierce, prophetic mom. Our God will hear us. After all, God already does.

— REFLECT —

What lessons about doing justice have you learned from your family? What lessons about doing justice do you hear in the Bible?

— READ —

Isaiah 1:17. Along with the prophet Micah, the prophet Isaiah makes very plain the requirements of our living.

— PRAY —

May the God of peace and power, who brings back the prophets of old to accompany us on our journeys today, make us all complete in everything good so that we may do God's will. May we live out the rest of our days to see farther, love deeper, and celebrate more beautifully. May we never, never, never turn away from terrible injustice but fight until our very last breath for equality, freedom, and justice for all. Amen.

40

IF NOT US, WHO?

Aaron Scott

> "'The rich,' said St. Vincent de Paul, 'should beg the poor to forgive us for the bread we bring them.'"
>
> —JONATHAN KOZOL

READ: JOB 24

Some passages of Scripture just speak so immediately to our daily struggles. The words of Job 24 bring vivid memories to my mind.

> They thrust the needy from the path
> and force all the poor of the land into hiding.

I see countless tents, tarps, and shacks lining freeway underpasses—up one day, then disappeared the next, removed by cities desperate to keep up appearances instead of keeping up with justice and mercy. I see signs turning parking lots and stoplights across the country into hostile territory: "No Loitering," "No Illegal Shopping Carts," "No Panhandling."

> The poor go about their labor of foraging food;
> the wasteland provides food for their children.

I see the anxious but deep and determined love of young parents I know—loving parents who will do anything to ensure their kids have food and shelter. Even when it means breaking some laws, even when it means swallowing their last shred of pride, even when it means risking their own safety, even when they're forced to make choices no parent should have to make.

> They gather fodder in the fields
> and glean in the vineyards of the wicked.

I see the faces of friends I've lost to prison or early death because somewhere along the way they had to resort to "gleaning in the vineyards of the wicked" by shoplifting from Walmart. The draconian punishment for such crimes of survival sent their chances of life spiraling down the drain.

> The fatherless child is snatched from the breast;
> the infant of the poor is seized for a debt.

I see hospital rooms where I've sat next to desolate young mothers as government workers pulled their newborns out of their arms. Because there is no access to healing and addiction recovery programs for poor people in most of this country. Because our government responds to homeless mothers by stealing their children instead of providing them with housing. Because empires have always preyed upon poor families, and our empire is no different.

> The groans of the dying rise from the city,
> and the souls of the wounded cry out for help.

I hear the anguished outbursts of so many sensitive, wise, complex people I know whose spirits have been callously trampled by violence. Economic violence has left them unsheltered and unprotected on the streets. Political violence has marked them as "criminal" because of poverty and disability. Social violence has turned them over to vigilantes who seek to "send a message" to other homeless people about their disposability.

> But God drags away the mighty by his power;
> though they become established, they have no assurance of life.
> He may let them rest in a feeling of security,
> but his eyes are on their ways.
> For a little while they are exalted, and then they are gone;
> they are brought low and gathered up like all others.

I hear the righteous outrage and fragile hope of the poor. When someone with some leverage or a camera asks "What do you want people to know about what it's like to be homeless?" the answer is clear: "Try walking a mile in our shoes. Try surviving like this even for a day. You'll find out you're no better than us."

Job 24 lays out so clearly that people are poor because systems have been set up to benefit the few and exploit the many. But this passage also raises the big question: why does God allow this to happen over and over again? From the days of Job to right now, why does God allow such suffering?

Every time we ask that question, God looks us right in the eyes and asks the same thing back: "Why do you, as my children, allow this to happen? Who among you will be willing to stand up for justice anew in each generation, before all the injustice gets so bad it takes everyone down? If not you, who?"

— REFLECT —

What do you think is God's biggest, wildest dream for people living in poverty? For people living paycheck to paycheck? For people who are homeless? What would it take to make that dream come true? How might that dream coming true change the world?

— READ —

Job 5:10–27. A man who has lost everything characterizes the many aspects of protection and security that God intends for all to have.

— PRAY —

Giver of all life, give us the courage and tenacity to restore dignity where it has been stolen, fairness where there is exploitation, and compassion where there is cruelty. Your justice cannot roll unless we do. Amen.

41

WOE TO YOU WHO PASS UNJUST LAWS

Charon Hribar

"Remember, we are dying in the streets. If we gotta
die this time. . . . I'm gonna die ripping the boards
down from these buildings. . . . I'm gonna die
because I want to live. . . . We gotta forget about
[taking over abandoned houses] being against the
law. . . . I'm dying in the streets. I think that should be
against the law."

—RONALD CASANOVA

READ: ISAIAH 10

In a study of vacant properties in New York City, researchers with Picture
the Homeless and Hunter College posed a crucial question: "Who benefits from vacancy in New York City, and does that benefit outweigh the
social and economic costs of the housing emergency?" The study revealed
that the reason people were homeless was not that there wasn't enough
housing. Instead, it demonstrated that "citywide, vacant property could

house the entire shelter population five times over." If this was true, then why did the city continue to spend $750 million a year to keep the homeless homeless?

Throughout the Bible, we are taught to care for those in need and to make the resources we have accessible to all. Luke 3:11 tells us, "Anyone who has two shirts should share with the one who has none, and anyone who has food should do the same." Matthew 25:35 declares, "For I was hungry and you gave me something to eat, I was thirsty and you gave me something to drink, I was a stranger and you invited me in." These texts are biblical mandates. They are not to be interpreted as acts of charity, but as God's judgment upon how we as a nation treat the least of these.

The prophets in the Bible warn us that we should not hoard our resources and that God has provided enough for all to enjoy abundance. Throughout the book of Isaiah, we are told that God will judge the rule of law that is used to devour the vineyard and loot the homes of the poor. God will destroy the rulers who crush God's people because of their own pride, selfishness, and greed.

If New York City has the material ability to house every single person who is currently without a home, we as people of faith must ask: What prevents it? What prevents it in cities and towns across the country? The prophet Isaiah was clear about where blame fell in his day. Isaiah 10:1–2 declares, "Woe to those who make unjust laws, to those who issue oppressive decrees, to deprive the poor of their rights and withhold justice from the oppressed of my people, making widows their prey and robbing the fatherless."

Isaiah helps us see it is unjust laws and policies that allow vacant properties to lie dormant and that promote speculation in gentrifying neighborhoods. Meanwhile, the people who once lived there are pushed into the streets. Laws allow families to be evicted from their homes in the middle of a global pandemic, while billionaires gain more and more wealth. Isaiah challenges us to see that those in power pass laws that produce suffering and misery for the poor and strip them of their basic rights.

It is our duty as people of faith to call out these unjust laws for what they are: violence and sin of the highest order. We must lift up the courageous actions of leaders like Ronald Casanova and declare that no one needs to be homeless in a time of great abundance. We must stand on the side of the millions of families across this country who face evictions and foreclosure. In a society that has the means to provide our basic rights, we must demand the right of every person to have health care, an adequate income, clean water, and a home.

We are taught to obey the law, under the assumption that the social structure in which we live is just. But when the economic system and the policies that protect it are designed to put corporate profits before people's lives, we, like Isaiah, must call out the policy violence that is taking place. We must be willing to proclaim that these laws are immoral and wrong.

— REFLECT —

What do you hear in the cries of Isaiah about laws used to justify the suffering and misery of our people? How is God calling us to take action in the face of structural sin? Where do you see violent structures governing your community and our society? What stops you from calling out immoral and wrong laws? And what sustains you in the effort to do so?

— READ —

Leviticus 25:8-55. This passage offers clear guidance on the laws and policies that will justly govern the abundance that God has provided.

— PRAY —

God of the poor, God of the exploited, God of justice and hope, bring forth a revolution of values in this country that might shine a light on your laws. The land you have created is an abundant resource provided so that all may thrive. Let greed and selfishness be banished as we remember that the earth belongs to you. And give us, the poor and dispossessed of this land, the strength and courage to be the stewards of justice, calling out unjust laws and ensuring that life and dignity become realities for all your creation. Amen.

42

IS THAT WHAT YOU CALL A FAST?

Nicholas Laccetti

> "Many of our young adults emerge from prison with skills in carpentry and culinary arts. We seek to hire them to rebuild the physical ruins of Grays Harbor County, to feed local people who are starving in the midst of natural abundance, and to always keep an eye on the horizon by studying and learning from other people's struggles for liberation. We believe that nobody's more qualified to be a 'restorer of streets to live in' (Isaiah 58) than a kid who's had to live on the streets for most of their life."
>
> —AARON SCOTT

READ: ISAIAH 58

These verses in Isaiah suggest that some people want to know God's ways but think they can do that at the same time that they have "forsaken the commands of . . . God." This reminds me so much of the United States, where many constantly try to determine God's motives, God's character, and what God wants of our lives. Many people "seem eager for God to come near" us, like the verse says. But too often this is an individual pursuit, or a Sunday pursuit at best. We, too, think we can draw near to God without following God's ordinances of justice.

I think about the actions one takes on a fast day, and what these verses in Isaiah say about what real fasting and prayer look like. When COVID-19 emerged, individuals took a lot of actions to try to flatten the curve of the disease. But like the idea that individual fasting and prayer are *the* way to get close to God, individual action wasn't enough. The Bible—from Deuteronomy to Isaiah to the words and actions of Jesus in the New Testament—suggests we need to pray and fast by connecting through collective action. In addition to individual actions, we need to *change our social policies* to match the "ordinance of God." In our era, that means policies that create a more just and equitable society—one that is able to withstand pandemics and natural disasters.

Isaiah 58:5 also reminds me of the falsity of much prayer and fasting: those supposedly humble but actually ostentatious displays of piety that only serve the self-interest of those in power. God says, "Is this the kind of fast I have chosen, only a day for people to humble themselves? Is it only for bowing one's head like a reed and for lying in sackcloth and ashes? Is that what you call a fast, a day acceptable to the Lord?"

During the era of COVID-19, corporations were quicker to respond to the new reality than our government was. It didn't take long for advertisements to talk about social distancing, thank our health care workers, or provide some motivational speech about how we'd "get through this together." But these were the same companies that made billions from the crisis. Many are the very companies that have failed to pay essential workers livable wages or keep working conditions safe.

Individual actions in times of crisis, including prayer and fasting, are good and important. But we shouldn't be asked to make these sacrifices alone, as individuals, with the false encouragement of corporations that claim to be humbling themselves but are actually oppressing their workers, evicting families from their homes, polluting the environment, profiting from health care, and paying off elected officials. This is not the kind of fast God chooses. Crises of poverty, racism, war, and environmental devastation might force us to make individual sacrifices—to bow our heads like reeds, in Isaiah's words, and to pray and fast. But those sacrifices are not what God is asking for unless they also join us together, in a powerful collective movement to enact justice in our world.

Aaron Scott, in the quote at the beginning of this reflection, describes the *collective* action being taken in Grays Harbor County, Washington, to restore the streets to live in. Chaplains on the Harbor is working with neighbors to rebuild their community, feed local people who are starving in the midst of abundance, and do political education. They are learning from other struggles for liberation to understand how to build a movement to challenge the unjust structures of our society.

These are projects of survival: actions that not only meet individual needs but fight to repair the breaches in our society so that everyone's needs are met. That is a true fast according to Isaiah, the fast that God chooses: collective action led by the poor "to loose the chains of injustice and untie the cords of the yoke, to set the oppressed free and break every yoke."

— REFLECT —

What are the "true fasts" in your community in the midst of crisis— the projects of survival that take care of individual needs while connecting us to collective action to change the structures of society and "repair the breach"?

— READ —

2 Timothy 3. In Paul's letter, he bids Timothy and us to hold on to Scripture and to recall true examples of faithful lives, describing falsity and deception lived by some others.

— PRAY —

Lord, let us make a true fast for you: to loose the bonds of injustice, to let the oppressed go free. Let us be the repairers of the breach in our broken society. Amen.

43

LAS POSADAS

Kenia Torres-Alcocer

"We must not seek the child Jesus in the pretty figures of our Christmas cribs. We must seek him among the undernourished children who have gone to bed at night with nothing to eat, among the poor newsboys who will sleep covered with newspapers in doorways."

—OSCAR ROMERO

READ: MATTHEW 2

I can still remember the planning of my first Las Posadas celebration. Las Posadas is a nine-day celebration of the nativity. From December 16 to 24, we reenact Mary and Joseph's search for lodging in Bethlehem, a story told in Matthew 2.

Union de Vecinos is an organization in a neighborhood in Los Angeles, east of the Los Angeles River, called Boyle Heights. This community is predominantly made up of immigrants from Mexico. On First Street you have Mariachi Plaza, where you can hear music playing. On Cesar Chavez Avenue are the street vendors selling delicious tamales, nopales, avocados, and fruit. There are nine Catholic churches in a 6.5-mile radius.

As an organizer, I consider my job to be not only organizing people around the issues impacting them (housing, pedestrian safety, environmental issues) but also learning from them. As I knock on doors, I use these questions to guide me through a conversation: If you could change one thing in your neighborhood, what would it be? What is one thing you miss from your neighborhood back in your home country?

The answers to the first question are expected: cleaner alleys, fixed potholes, more lighting, safer streets and crosswalks, stop signs, traffic lights, and habitable homes. The answers to the second question are more surprising, because they are so similar no matter where the person is from. They miss how on their block back home, people knew each other and would help each other out. The women on their block would all come out at the same time of day to sweep the street and gossip. They miss gathering with their neighbors on Día de la Virgen de Guadalupe to pray the rosary for those who have passed away. And they miss getting together to plan Las Posadas.

So at one of our planning meetings with Union de Vecinos, we discussed the following questions: What is Las Posadas? Who is Las Posadas for? Why do we celebrate it? What is the significance of us celebrating Las Posadas here in this country? How do we see ourselves reflected in Las Posadas?

The answers to these questions were so simple, yet so profound. Las Posadas is for *us*. It is a reminder of the coming of baby Jesús and of how María and José traveled to give Jesús a better life. We want to celebrate Las Posadas here in this country so we can be connected to our traditions. Like María and José, we have all migrated to give our children a better life. Just like them, we ended up not in the castle but in a poor community.

Jesús was born in a stable with horses, sheep, and pigs; we are in homes with roaches, rats, and lead. But even in those conditions, Jesús receives gifts from the three kings: gold, incense, and myrrh. We too have new gifts that we want to celebrate. We have community, unity, and the victories accomplished throughout the year.

The first Las Posadas procession is led by two children dressed up as María and José and carrying a baby. Along the route we stop at places where we are organizing, and people share a poem, a skit, or a testimony. Some tell stories of why they migrated, or about their landlord who refuses to fix up their building, or about elected officials who don't want to meet their demands. At each stop we sing *"En el nombre del cielo hos pido posada"* ("In the name of the heavens we ask for refuge"). On the third stop we enter and there is food, a piñata for the children, candy, and music. This is a true celebration of the birth of a man who came to teach us how to save ourselves.

Las Posadas for Union de Vecinos has become a time for reflection and celebration. As immigrants, as tenants, and as the poor and dispossessed, we are not just looking for empty Christmas celebrations. We are seeking our God: the God of the poor. We are finding Jesus in ourselves and those who are with us in the struggle for a more just society.

— REFLECT —

Where would be some of the stops along your Las Posadas procession? Where are María, José, and Jesús today? How is God our refuge?

— READ —

Deuteronomy 10:17-20. This Scripture offers a loving recollection of the God of the poor.

— PRAY —

God, in the same way you guided María and José in their migration journey to Bethlehem, we ask you to guide the journeys of all migrants and refugees who are currently crossing borders to have a better life. Help us liberate ourselves from the tyrants who, like Herod, misuse their power and position to oppress us. Guide our movement to end poverty, systemic racism, ecological devastation, and the war economy. We ask you to give us the strength of María and José to embrace this task, for it is through your son, Jesucristo, that we learn to stand up to empire. Amen.

44

SONG OF REVOLUTIONARY MOTHERS

Savina J. Martin

> "I picked the group that prayed before their meetings because I knew that without God on our side-we did not stand a chance."
>
> —DOTTIE STEVENS

READ: LUKE 1:46-56

Mary's Song, also known as the Magnificat and found in Luke 1, speaks of the spirit and the power of God. In this canticle, Mary speaks of how her soul magnifies the Lord and how God regarded the lowly maidservant. She informs us that generations to come will call her blessed.

German theologian Dietrich Bonhoeffer recognized the subversive nature of Mary's Song. He spoke these words in a sermon during Advent in 1933: "The song of Mary is the oldest Advent hymn. It is at once the most passionate, the wildest, one might even say the most revolutionary Advent hymn ever sung. This is not the gentle, tender, dreamy Mary whom we sometimes see in paintings. . . . This song has none of the sweet, nostalgic, or even playful tones of some of our Christmas carols."

The government of Guatemala in the 1980s also recognized the subversive nature of Mary's Song. The government found Mary's proclamation—that God is especially concerned for the poor—to be so dangerous and revolutionary that it banned any public recitation of Mary's words.

Among those who saw their own story and hope in Mary's Song in the United States was Dottie Stevens, a revolutionary mother from East Boston and a longtime organizer of the poor. Dottie was married at age sixteen and decided to leave home, just as our beloved revolutionary sister Mary did. Facing ridicule as a young wife, she discovered a place to belong among the rank and file of the National Welfare Rights Union. She referred to her decision to join the movement as her political baptism.

Dottie passed away in June 2014 after a battle with cancer. She had been a fighter, survivor, and organizer of the poor most of her life. Courageous in the face of poverty, she fought for many decades for the rights of the poor and dispossessed. She worked with and among many leaders across many fronts of struggle. She stood up to the state apparatus as she raised her fist and banner against injustices done to the poor. Dottie was an artist, an activist, a musician who played the piano, and a mother and wife. She advocated for those who were unfairly treated, those who were let down and left out. She spoke at countless meetings and rallies all over the country for decades, shouting "Up and out poverty, now!"

Just like Mary, Dottie was speaking a song of her time and of the things to come. We know that the poor are blamed for their own poverty. The unhoused are demonized for being homeless, hungry, and in need of rest. And we know that we, the people, have the power to change the course of our lives, with justice and mercy on our side. Let us be reminded of the songs we sing as we build power and take control of our narrative. Let us be called to action in spirit and in truth, joining both the revolutionary mothers of old and those of our time, who sing their song like Mary did.

The Magnificat is a song of salvation, with political, economic, and social dimensions that cannot be blunted. Dottie was an abuse survivor, a teenage wife, and a freedom fighter for justice and mercy for the poor. Through her work on welfare rights, Dottie fought for mothers to be able to put food on the table and have heat and hot water during the winter months.

In her song, Mary speaks to the poor, the hungry, the homeless. People in every society hear the blessing in this canticle.

— REFLECT —

Why have the words of Mary been repressed throughout history? What in them is dangerous?

— READ —

1 Samuel 2:1–10. This passage is known as Hannah's Song. Like Hannah, we can pray out of our anguish and grief, deeply troubled, awaiting the birth of what we desire most: justice. Like Mary and like Hannah, we can also pray out of praise and confidence. Knowing God is faithful to lift up the poor, we can be confident that justice will be born.

— PRAY —

My soul glorifies the Lord and my spirit rejoices in God, my Savior! God, you know my pain and my plight. You scatter the proud. You bring rulers down from their thrones. But the hungry are filled with good things. The humble are lifted up. This promise from you, God, is written on my heart. Amen.

PART VI
THE BIRTH OF
A MOVEMENT

45

MIDWIVES WHO SAY NO

Tammy Rojas

"There is a hegemonic form of violence that has become normalized. It doesn't always bleed or make news headlines, but it's the violence baked into the way that we live every day, that we rarely ever face, because it might be too much to do so. There is violence being done to us, and the invisibilized violence *we participate in just by virtue of being part of the system that we live in.*"

—NIJMIE DZURINKO

READ: EXODUS 1

Growing up in Lancaster, Pennsylvania, known as a conservative religious county, I was taught by my father's side of the family that whatever suffering I experienced and whatever trauma was inflicted on me were God's will. I couldn't bring myself to say prayers of praise to a God who apparently was not only okay with me living in poverty and experiencing abuse but had *willed* it to be so. Instead, my prayers were mostly pleas for freedom from the suffering that I and the people I cared about were experiencing.

But I experienced a political and spiritual awakening in 2016. I realized that I couldn't just stand by silently anymore, and I began to look into what

I could do to make a difference. It's because of my deep love and respect for all people that I fight as hard as I do now against systems of oppression.

In 2017, I found a home with Put People First! PA, which is a part of the Pennsylvania Poor People's Campaign and gives voice to everyday people across the state who are struggling to meet basic needs.

One of our goals has been to keep a hospital from closing in our city. When the University of Pittsburgh Medical Center (UPMC) announced the planned closure of St. Joseph's Hospital, we, as an organized front of the poor and dispossessed of all backgrounds, took action and fought back against the closure. For me, fighting for St. Joseph's Hospital means I'm fighting for my mother and grandmother, who taught me the values of strength and love. Fighting for this hospital is fighting for my grandfather, who showed me the value of hard work and dedication to one's family and community. For us, fighting for this hospital is fighting to save the legacy of the entire working class. It's our blood, sweat, and tears that made St. Joseph's Hospital into a spiritual place—a place that will live in the hearts of many for years to come.

In Exodus 1, we learn of Pharaoh's intent to destroy the gains of the Hebrew people and co-opt the midwives' power. Pharaoh commands the midwives to kill Hebrew-born sons and let the girls live. The midwives chose to obey the law of God and disobey the law of Pharaoh.

The $21 billion UPMC system is the pharaoh of health care in Pennsylvania. Those of us uniting to stand up against it are the midwives. Through grassroots, multiracial, and nonpartisan organizing efforts, the poor and dispossessed—accompanied by some leaders in the faith community—chose to obey the law of God and stand up to Pharaoh. Healthcare is a human right, we said. Our elected officials and other faith leaders chose to obey the law of Pharaoh and betray us.

In our fight to save the hospital, we had many wins and some losses. But we came together to fight the injustices of our system, and because of that, the hospital still stands. We are still fighting back against the rezoning and redevelopment plans proposed by UPMC and developers, and whether we ultimately save St. Joseph's Hospital remains to be seen. Either way, however, we know the system of oppression still exists, so "midwives" across Pennsylvania must continue to unite to take down "Pharaoh." We must win health care as a human right for all in our state.

The only way we can change the system of oppression we live under is for all of us to come together. We may be taught division, but we can unlearn it. We can fight back against it and show that love of all people will be what saves us.

Because of the distorted Christian narrative I was taught most of my life, I used to wrestle with believing in God. Memories of abusive incidents still haunt me. But I've grown through this movement in many ways. This movement has been restoring my faith in God and deepening my understanding of the teachings of Jesus Christ.

There are no more Sunday masses inside the walls of St. Joseph's Hospital, but Father Michael's final sermon inside the chapel there is instilled in our memories forever. He assured those in attendance on that day that "although the future of the property and building is uncertain, St. Joe's spirit will always be on College Avenue: its roots are deep within the property's soil and foundation and God dwells within."

God dwells within the walls of closed rural hospitals and pours onto the streets with those demanding health care as a human right. There are midwives saying no to the injustice of killing babies and midwives saying no to the denial of health care. It is through nonviolent direct action that we can overcome empire.

— REFLECT —

How and when in your life have you had to choose between the law of God and the law of Pharaoh?

— READ —

Matthew 19:23-26, 2 Corinthians 11:13-15, Mark 7:9-13, and 1 Samuel 17. These Scriptures provide examples of the false choices sometimes set before us and build our resolve to fight for the law of God (over empire).

— PRAY —

Lord, help me believe that you are with me even when I'm unsure whether you are. Amen.

46

WHOSE LAW AND WHOSE ORDER?

Solita Alexander Riley

> "Where justice is denied, where poverty is enforced, where ignorance prevails, and where any one class is made to feel that society is an organized conspiracy to oppress, rob and degrade them, neither persons nor property will be safe."
>
> —FREDERICK DOUGLASS

READ: EXODUS 20

Law and order. We hear this phrase a lot, and it raises a lot of questions. Who or what is the law protecting? What order is being demanded and kept in place? Who benefits from enforcing quality-of-life crimes, like bans on panhandling and noise ordinances? Is it code for racist policy and white male domination? What are the principles undergirding the law? Does the law serve the privileged few or the common good? Does the law provide ideals for our collective betterment?

I am an immigrant woman raising a Black male child in the United States, and I have real questions about who the law protects and what interests it serves. Both the historical and present record show that far too often the law does not protect from harm but contributes to it. This is true even when laws are developed as a means of recompense.

Yet I know my family and I, this nation, and all of creation are subject to a higher law: God's law. It is in that law that true freedom, security, and life itself exist. The law of God establishes an order of equality,
love, and regard for one another. The Ten Commandments provide a
means by which we flourish individually and collectively.

We find the Ten Commandments in the book of Exodus. It is very
important to consider the biblical context, because the setting helps us
understand all the "do nots." In moving into liberation from slavery
under Pharaoh, the ancient Israelites had to heal from both individual
injury and historical trauma. They had to become whole people again,
and they also had to become *a* whole people. They had to fashion a
new and healthy society, separate and different from the death dealing of
Pharaoh's empire. But how? What would be the backbone of their society?
What would be the pillars of strength to hold up this people? What was
the law and order?

Enter the Ten Commandments: a path to identity and social wholeness. It strikes me as significant that Moses—who had witnessed countless atrocities committed against people and who was drawn into violence
himself—was entrusted to deliver this higher law and order.

The first set of commandments is about our allegiance to God. God is
claiming the people, their oppression, and their liberation, and God wants
to be claimed by the people. Right relationship to God is key in the first
four commandments. The second set of commandments is about our life
together: about being in right relationship with each other.

To fashion this whole society, the people had to center their relationship with God, which meant they had to deeply understand what God
is about. The first commandment reminded them that God liberates
people—that God is about the end of oppression. No person or thing is
higher than God or can take God's place. So whatever form this new
society was to take, love surely had to be its primary ethic.

The fourth commandment reminded people of the ways that God per-
forms work, a sharp contrast to the ways of work under Pharaoh. God created, giving each aspect of creation work to do, and then God rested. So
the people needed to be mindful about their work—the new order needed
to include fair labor for all and rest for all. As someone concerned with
labor practices and involved in job creation efforts, I find great significance in this Sabbath commandment. It speaks to the need to respect all
people, all animals, all creation. All that we and they are able to produce

is to be honored and cherished. This implies fair compensation and mandates that we leave time for rejuvenation.

The remaining verses remind us that not only are we to honor God, but we are to honor life itself, from those who give us life (our parents) to those who live by our side (our neighbors). No community or society can stand unless all lives are honored, are deemed sacred, are valued. The devaluing of life is the very thing that can wreck a community. The killing of the Hebrew babies, the oppressive labor required of the enslaved Hebrews: these were the beginning of Pharaoh's undoing.

Disregard for life has been the undoing of the United States as well. But it's not too late. Many prophets are crying out that someone's hurting their people, that life matters. They show the ways that laws are killing us. They demonstrate that many laws allow only a privileged few to prevail through ill-gotten—and often legal—gains.

So we call not for law and order, but for laws of a new order. We call for a law based on life-affirming principles. We know that God has called us into this kind of rule. If God said it's meant to be so, it will be so.

— REFLECT —

What laws are killing us? What laws are healing us and keeping our society together? What new laws are needed to ensure you and your community live fully? How is God calling you to declare these laws?

— READ —

Luke 10. Love God and love your neighbor as yourself; everything hinges on these two commandments.

— PRAY —

Holy One, thank you that your reign is held together by life-affirming principles. Thank you for wanting each of us, our communities, and our societies to live and flourish. Help us to live in right relationship with you and with others. Grant us the continued boldness and faith to advocate for and live out laws that establish your just order. Amen.

47

SURVIVAL ECONOMICS

Sarah Monroe

> "Here is what we seek: a compassion that can stand in awe at what the poor have to carry rather than stand in judgment at how they carry it."
>
> —GREG BOYLE

READ: RUTH 2-3

The world of the poor is full of the contradictions of trauma and survival. Perhaps nowhere in the Bible is that more evident than in the book of Ruth. It is quite easy, especially in the Christian tradition, to judge the decisions poor people make in order to survive. I grew up in a poor, majority-white community where we were taught, as most poor whites are, that when people lose everything, it is their fault.

The story in the book of Ruth centers around two women, a widow named Naomi and her daughter-in-law Ruth, who make a series of morally ambiguous decisions in order to survive. In *The Peoples' Bible*, Wilda Gafney suggests that Ruth and Orpah, the two Moabite daughters-in-law in the story, were likely kidnapped and forced into marriage, based on the Hebrew verbs used. They are an unlikely family, moving from place to place in the Fertile Crescent during a period of political unrest and famine. When Naomi loses her sons and her husband and returns to Palestine,

Ruth goes with her, an outsider and immigrant to the culture and God of the Hebrews. They create their own family and community of solidarity, dedicated to each other's survival in a harsh world.

Ruth is determined to keep Naomi and herself housed and fed. She takes advantage of a system of charity in the Hebrew world that allowed hungry people to gather leftover grain. When she gains the notice of her mother-in-law's wealthy relative, she thanks him for his kindness, and he also ensures that she stays safe from predatory men. With the help of her mother-in-law, she approaches this wealthy kinsman while he is drunk at night. The text does not say that Ruth attempts to trade sex for security, but it can be read as implying that.

This attempt succeeds for Ruth—the immigrant, the poor widow, perhaps even the sex worker—and she becomes the celebrated great-grandmother of King David. As happens so often in the Bible, people with messed-up pasts and great struggles become the leaders and founders of movements.

As in the time of Ruth, the contemporary world of the poor is filled with impossible choices. I remember my sense of deep shame during my own bout with homelessness and the lengths I went to in order to hide my struggle. I now work as a pastor to people experiencing homelessness in Aberdeen, Washington, a postindustrial logging town on the far edge of the West Coast. With close to 50 percent of people on public assistance, more than 75 percent of children qualifying for free lunch, and one out of sixteen people homeless, our town carries countless stories of people's savage and dire struggle to survive.

Many locals, even pastors, judge people experiencing poverty, home-lessness, and the addiction that often comes with them. Many neighbor-hoods have drug houses and flophouses, where twenty or thirty people may live off and on, trading whatever they can for a space on the floor or a couch. There is a harsh solidarity on the streets, where people take care of each other—but also fight each other for every scrap of food or clothes and every pair of Jordans.

The young women I know on the streets believe that there are more homeless women than men. Women are less likely to inherit or own prop-erty, less likely to be on a lease, and usually more dependent on relation-ships for protection. The women from Aberdeen's streets have seen hell: they have tried to revive friends who have overdosed, lost loved ones in front of their eyes, and nursed loved ones in muddy tents and vehicles without access to decent medical care. I don't think I know a woman who has not been raped or assaulted. I know very few women who have not done time for poverty-related offenses or drug crimes.

In the middle of a daily struggle to survive, I have found extraordinary courage. I have seen young people care for each other in tents on the banks of a river. I have seen people go out of their way to make sure an elder survives the night or gets to their next meal. Even when a local resident throws explosives at their tents, or city officials call them a "public nuisance," they find the strength to go on.

The women I know survive, like Ruth did. They survive despite lack of health care, lack of treatment, constant criminalization, and hunger and cold and deep trauma. They are my heroes.

— REFLECT —

What are ways that you judge yourself or the community in which you live or serve? How can you see people's struggles in light of their courage instead of solely their mistakes? How can you see your own struggles in light of your own courage instead of your mistakes?

— READ —

Luke 6:20-26, Luke 7:36-50, and Luke 15. Jesus teaches us that those who are demeaned and outcast—those who may make mistakes and those held in negative judgment by others—are actually blessed by God.

— PRAY —

God, give us compassion and awe for those who show strength and courage. Forgive us for the times we have stood in judgment. Help us find the strength and wisdom of Ruth in meeting our own needs and the needs of our community as we work for a world where the needs of all are fully met. Amen.

48

THE EMPIRE'S RECEIPTS

C. Wess Daniels

> "The poor are the ones who constitute a despised and culturally marginalized race. At best, the poor are present in statistics, but they do not appear in society with proper names. We do not know the name of the poor. They are and remain anonymous. The poor ones are socially insignificant, but not so to God."
>
> —GUSTAVO GUTIÉRREZ

READ: REVELATION 18

The last part of a transaction at a store is usually the cashier asking whether you'd like a receipt. I usually decline, trying to save a little paper and slow the trash buildup in my pockets. But a receipt is an important thing. A budget tells you how you *intend* to spend your money; a receipt tells you how you actually spent it. It says something about what we prioritize and value. How we prioritize our spending shows what we value.

Now imagine having access to years' worth of receipts from a government. Again, not the budget—we have all seen the budgets. The $30,000 line item in the budget for a senator's travel is like viewing the moon

through a telescope. But the stack of receipts showing how the senator
actually spent that $30,000? That's like walking on the moon.

In Revelation, we find a two-thousand-year-old "receipt." Revelation
18:11–13 offers a detailed account of what is known to scholars as Rome's
cargo list—that which the empire spent its money on.

Revelation means "an unmasking." What the pages of this book reveal
is that empire is a set of oppressive practices and distorted theology that
stand in opposition to God. In this chapter, the writer of Revelation
announces, "Fallen! Fallen is Babylon the Great!" Babylon, here and
elsewhere in Revelation, is a stand-in for the Roman Empire. This cargo
list—the receipt of the Roman Empire—reveals the underlying sin. Given
access to documents so often hidden from public view, we see why Revelation 18 is one of the most damning passages on empire in the entire
New Testament.

Let's take a hard look at how the Roman Empire spent its money.
When we read Revelation 18:11–13, we see a list that reveals opulence and
luxury. Most of the items in the early parts of this list are not necessities,
and they are certainly not items to which the poor have ever had access.
These are items of wealth and excess, gathered with the empire's power.

As we get to the bottom of the list, it takes an even more horrific turn.
Not only does empire flaunt its riches and serve the 1 percent; it exploits
all of creation, animals, and "human beings sold as slaves" (18:13). The
Roman Empire doesn't stop with spices and cloth; it builds its economy on
the exploited bodies of the enslaved the same way that every empire has
and does. Here within the Christian Scriptures, written in approximately
90 CE, God's sheer disgust and judgment upon this system are clear.

Christians throughout history who refuse the teachings of this text
and pit themselves against the "insignificant" ones, as Gustavo Gutiérrez
says, pit themselves against God.

If we were to look at the receipts of the wealthy today, what would we
find? They show tax breaks for billionaires while essential workers are
underpaid, lack basic social safety nets like health care, and often have to
work multiple jobs just to pay rent and put food on the table. Tax documents show that Donald Trump paid $0 in taxes in ten of fifteen recent
years, and in 2016–2017 he paid just $750. One political advisor pointed
out in the *New York Times* that "In 2017, a single worker without children
who made $18,000 would have paid $760 in federal income tax." The
empire's receipts show politicians using $75,000 haircuts as tax write-offs
while poor and low-income families face unemployment and evictions.

In God's vision, there is a different world, a different system, a radical redistribution in which no one is overlooked. Everyone can have enough if no one hoards resources and opportunities. This receipt looks like the poor organizing against the empire and creating projects of survival.

NC Raise Up, an organization of low-wage workers in North Carolina, saw families struggling with hunger. So they created Fed Up, a project of survival in the tradition of the Black Panther breakfast program. Each week community members come together to distribute fresh local produce and other donated food to more than eight hundred families. This is not simply an act of charity; it is an act of solidarity and organizing, because they hand out both food and knowledge. Neighbors are organizing their community to address the underlying injustices that lead to hungry families.

Fed Up demonstrates a great generosity: of time, food, and solidarity. This is what the receipt of God's kingdom looks like.

— REFLECT —

If you had access to the receipts of those in power in your community, what do you think you would find?

— READ —

Ezekiel 7. This passage challenges us to look through God's eyes at our community's receipts.

— PRAY —

God, we ask for judgment upon those who live in the lap of luxury while people starve, die from lack of health care, and, like you, have no place to lay their heads. May there be swift and stern judgment on all those who exploit others for their benefit. And may your generosity and peace be with those who take care of their community members by whatever means they have at their disposal. Amen.

49

WHAT THE WAY LOOKS LIKE

Tonny H. Algood

> "True compassion is more than flinging a coin to a beggar. It comes to see that an edifice which produces beggars needs restructuring."
>
> —MARTIN LUTHER KING JR.

READ: ACTS 2:43-47

I often wondered what life among the early believers in Christ was really like. In Acts 4:34–35, we are told that they owned everything in common and worshipped and broke bread together. There were no beggars among them! Jesus had taught them how to restructure the "edifice which produces beggars," in Martin Luther King Jr.'s words. They did not follow the way of the Roman Empire, which depended on brutal slavery, violence, and oppression to survive.

Jesus came and taught us the way to live in a community of love for each other—what King called "the beloved community." As a matter of fact, the early followers of Jesus were not called Christians but were known as people of "the Way." They followed the way of living that Jesus had taught them through his words, actions, and deeds. And the followers of Jesus grew in numbers and thrived!

In the year 100 CE, there were twenty-five thousand followers of Jesus. By the year 310 CE, right before Constantine entered the scene, there were up to twenty million. How could this happen? During this period Christianity was an illegal religion, and its adherents were often severely persecuted. They did not have any church buildings. They did not yet have the full Scriptures. They did not have seeker-sensitive services, paid pastors, youth groups, worship bands, seminaries, or commentaries.

I believe that this phenomenal growth under these conditions was a confirmation of the way Jesus taught us to live. It was so powerful, and so good, that the church became a real threat to the empire. There is an old saying: "Keep your friends close, and keep your enemies closer." This is just what Constantine did when he made Christianity the official religion of the Roman Empire.

The Christianity of empire is used to sanction wars of aggression and the exploitation of the poor and oppressed. The religion of empire has been used to justify genocide of Native Americans; implement the most brutal form of slavery that the world has ever witnessed; steal land from Mexico; and exploit people and natural resources of the Global South. The religion of empire seizes land and housing in the name of profits for a few. It destroys the very environments we need to survive. It leaves in its wake death and destruction. And in the United States, the religion of empire has built the largest military power in the world, leaving death, devastation, and poverty in its wake.

Millions in our country and throughout the world are homeless. More than 140 million people are living in poverty in what is claimed to be the richest country in the world. This can't be the "kingdom of God on earth" that Jesus taught us to pray for and to build.

So exactly what happened to the Way? Did it die when the religion of empire was birthed? No. It has lived on and has expressed itself in movements and leaders who have struggled for justice throughout history.

The Way appeared in the abolitionist movement to defeat slavery and the continuing fight to defeat the vestiges of Jim Crow and systemic racism. The Way expresses itself in the movement to eliminate systemic poverty so no one will be in need. The Way is found in the movement to provide housing for everyone. (There are three vacant, habitable houses for every person who will be sleeping on the streets in the United States tonight.) The early followers of the Way broke bread together, and no one was hungry. (Today, 46 percent of the food that is produced for consumption goes into the garbage at the end of the day, while people go hungry.)

The Way that Jesus taught is revolutionary because it challenges the religion of empire. The Way restructures the edifice upon which the religion of empire depends. Flinging a coin to a beggar is charity; this is what the churches of the empire teach its members to do. Charity is easy and doesn't have to hurt us at all. We can give what we want, to whom we want, when we want, if we want.

Justice, on the other hand, brings the structural changes that will make charity unnecessary. Justice restructures the edifice. But justice always comes with a sacrifice. The sacrifice of joining a movement may take the form of lost relationships with family or friends, loss of income or physical well-being, incarceration, or even loss of one's life.

Of course, this should not come as a surprise to those of us who follow the Way of a dark-skinned, brown-eyed Palestinian Jew who showed us how to overcome the religion of the empire.

— REFLECT —

What do you think the kingdom of God would look like on earth? How do you see it appearing now? What structural changes would you like to see made in our country today?

— READ —

2 Corinthians 8-9. The early church provides a glimpse of alternatively structured community.

— PRAY —

God, from the time of the prophets through today, you have called on us to do justice, and to love kindness, and to walk humbly with you. We ask that you give us the courage, wisdom, and—most of all—the love for others and for the world necessary to live out the way that you have taught us. Amen.

50

BAND-AIDS OR JUSTICE

Carolyn Jean Foster

"This movement is trying to be like a doctor to this nation. A good doctor that will tell you when you're really sick! A good doctor that will not apply Band-Aids to wounds. We cannot accept these Band-Aids anymore."

—WILLIAM J. BARBER II

READ: JEREMIAH 6

I learned early in life that the place where you live matters. I grew up in a neighborhood called Smithfield, a few miles west of downtown Birmingham, Alabama. It was the Black side of town. Many of the students who participated in the 1963 Children's March organized by Rev. James Bevel, an advisor to Rev. Dr. Martin Luther King, lived in the neighborhood. Smithfield became known as Dynamite Hill because it was the frequent target of bombings by the Ku Klux Klan.

Back then, the place where you lived, especially for African Americans, was dictated by the powers of segregationists and systemic injustices like racism and poverty. In fact, the framers of the 1901 Alabama State Constitution proudly proclaimed that their intention was "to establish white supremacy by law." Those words still stand, although in 2020 the state finally voted to remove some offensive language. In my childhood, the provisions of the Constitution disenfranchised most African Americans, as well as thousands of poor whites.

The ravages of segregation, and the tentacles of poverty that it caused, still have a firm grip on many communities of color. Where you live dictates educational resources, access to public transportation and health care, and employment opportunities. Where you live determines whether you can easily obtain fresh fruits and vegetables and whether you breathe fresh air or have clean water flowing from your kitchen tap. Where you live determines whether you can easily exercise your right to vote. Place matters.

The experience of living in a segregated neighborhood that was terrorized by white supremacists led to my work as a social justice advocate, community organizer, and antiracism workshop facilitator. I work every day with people who are victims of systemic racism and poverty. Some live in poor housing conditions, breathe toxic air, and lack public transportation to get to doctor appointments or other essential services. They disproportionately suffer from asthma, bronchitis, hypertension, and diabetes because they live in neighborhoods surrounded by industrial plants that produce toxic fumes and soil contaminants.

Place matters—and the people who live in those places matter, too!

Poor people are blamed and scapegoated for their situation; they are ignored and manipulated by the people elected to represent them. We must work for complete restoration and healing for people whose wounds are deep and systemic in nature. Band-Aid solutions warned about in Jeremiah are not good enough. Bryan Stevenson, executive director of the Equal Justice Initiative, says, "The opposite of poverty is not wealth; the opposite of poverty is justice."

So what would justice look like for the poor? In Luke 14:7–14, Jesus shows us. Having arrived at a wedding banquet, he notices how the powerful and affluent are seating themselves in places of prominence at the banquet table, and in this parable he uses the table as a metaphor for the kingdom of God. Jesus says the place of honor is for the host to decide, and he suggests these guests humble themselves and take a seat of less prominence. It is much better, he teaches, to be invited up to a place of honor than to be asked to step down.

Then Jesus turns his attention to the host of the banquet. The host, he says, should have instead invited those who were poor, disabled, and blind. By inviting only the rich, the host set up a quid pro quo scenario: I will scratch your back now so you can scratch mine later. But if he had invited to his table the poor and marginalized, who could not repay the favor, that invitation would have bent toward humility, equity, and inclusivity.

Justice looks like poor people at the table, having meaningful conversations with equal voice to articulate solutions to problems that directly impact them. All too often people in power pose solutions to systemic issues without engaging people who are directly affected. People who live in poverty know the solutions that would alleviate their suffering; they just do not have the resources. They need to be at the table. Place matters.

Band-Aid solutions can slow the immediate bleed of wounds caused by systemic poverty and racism. But for any wound to be healed, it must be lanced, cleansed, and treated at the source. The healing balm for the wounds of systemic poverty is restorative justice.

Justice for those entrapped by systemic poverty looks like admitting the hurt, acknowledging the cause of the pain, and making it right. If you want to help heal the wounds of those suffering, come and stand alongside them. Follow their lead: listen, learn, and work.

— REFLECT —

Recall a time that you realized your "place" either benefited you or was a barrier to you. What did you notice? Whom do you need to sit next to at the table? What would you hope to say or hear once seated?

— READ —

Luke 14:7-14. The story of Jesus inviting the poor and sick to the wedding banquet tells a story of justice—with the poor not simply as placeholders but as active agents of change.

— PRAY —

God, bless me with discernment to ask hard questions concerning the cause of systemic poverty. Move me with compassion for those who are hurting, suffering, oppressed, and vulnerable. Bring restorative justice. Amen.

51

SAME SIN, DIFFERENT DAY

Aaron Scott

They may take my home
They may scatter my belongings
But they will surely burn in hell.
For whoever is no man's keeper
Is no man at all
But a beast, a tool of the devil.

—ANONYMOUS, "UNTITLED"

READ: ISAIAH 5:8–10

In Aberdeen, Washington, the public works department demolished the city's largest homeless encampment. While there is plenty of vitriol toward unhoused people in Aberdeen (and nationwide), an encampment sweep is the kind of brutality that city officials are good at making sound mundane. Their rhetoric was couched in terms of public safety, or public nuisance, or taxpayer concerns. It's a big headache for the mayor; it's a real eyesore that somebody's got to clean up; we've got to keep attracting tourists; blah blah blah. The boringness of the rhetoric intentionally obscures the violence.

What is the demolition of a homeless camp like? To the mayor, it is a PR stunt in an election year. To the police chief, it is a potential publicity nightmare. To the city attorney, it is a pain in the rear. To local property and business owners, it is a long-awaited cause for celebration.

To the poor, it is an apocalypse. It is exile. It is an act of war.

It is fourteen police cars pulling up to a small string of plywood shacks and tents just to serve the eviction notices. It is bulldozers trying to move in on structures while people are still sleeping inside them. It is watching the homestead you built with your own hands, out of the scraps and garbage other people threw away, be snatched up and crushed by a roaring excavator, against your will, with no other place to turn.

In the richest country on earth.

Poor people are not the problem. A society that isn't even satisfied with poor people living in shacks but must also relentlessly attack and displace them is the problem. In recognizing the authority of poor people, we have to listen to poor people. We have to hear homeless folks' first-hand accounts of how our cities are investing in expensive militarization directed against them instead of investing in the things that could save lives, like affordable housing and health care.

What would Isaiah say if he stood at that camp on the banks of the Chehalis River, surrounded by cop cars, construction equipment, and weeping, cussing homeless people? I think Isaiah would say, "Same sin, different day." Isaiah might sound a bit like the writer of the poem at the beginning of this chapter—one of the displaced residents of the Aberdeen encampment—after he watched the city bulldoze his small cabin. But Isaiah might also say that if we are to have any hope of eventually turning things around and rebuilding from the ashes, we will find it among people who are already figuring out how to survive the apocalypse every day.

Chaplains on the Harbor, a mission station of the Episcopal Church, eventually participated in two federal lawsuits against the city of Aberdeen for its treatment of homeless people. Rev. Sarah Monroe stood as plaintiff alongside ten homeless residents of the camp. Though the original camp was demolished, the plaintiffs won damages and a new city-funded campsite, and they set federal precedent with their victory, even as their local struggle continues.

Here are some lines from Rev. Sarah's statement on the first lawsuit:

I am a priest. I have been pastoring the people in this camp for five years. I do everything from drive people to the hospital, to prayer, to taking people to social service appointments, to performing last rites when people die here. . . . I have continued to visit people, even though I have been denied a permit, and am petitioning the court to prevent the city from arresting me. Homeless people have a constitutionally protected right to freedom of religious expression. I have a constitutionally protected right to my freedom of religious expression, which includes serving the poor and the sick and the hungry. The city's actions are a clear attempt to isolate, marginalize, and further criminalize people who have already been pushed to the edge of existence in this community. I consider it my duty as an American citizen and my vocation as a priest to stand against this.

Same sin, different day: encampment after encampment razed, while the rich add "house to house," as Isaiah bemoans. But with each day also comes the bravery, resourcefulness, and faithfulness of those who refuse the bulldozer and the wicked march of oblivion, with God at their side.

— REFLECT —

Do you see those in power adding "house to house" and joining "field to field" (Isaiah 5:8) today? Where? What feelings come up when you notice this? How can you put those feelings to use?

— READ —

Psalm 147:1–6. This psalm praises an all-powerful God and shows the many ways God is at the side of the exiled and brokenhearted.

— PRAY —

God, we know you made this world big enough for all of us to have a safe place to lay our heads each night. Protect all of us who may be sleeping unsheltered tonight—and show us how we can come together to demand homes for all your children. Amen.

52

HOW TO SURVIVE A PANDEMIC

Marco Saavedra

"Behold here comes the dreamer, come now, let us kill him and we shall see what becomes of his dreams. (Genesis 37:19, 20)"

—WORDS ETCHED ONTO A SLAB OF CONCRETE STAINED BY THE BLOOD OF MARTIN LUTHER KING JR.'S MURDEROUS GUNSHOT WOUND, MEMPHIS, TENNESSEE

READ: GENESIS 47

How do you survive a pandemic?

My family was displaced from our indigenous village, San Miguel Ahuehuetitlan, by hunger, poverty, and free trade agreements in 1992. In 2009, amid the Great Recession, my parents opened their own restaurant, La Morada, in the South Bronx, one of the poorest neighborhoods in the country. As undocumented immigrants, they had been continually laid off, and so they decided to start their own restaurant.

When my neighborhood became an epicenter of the global COVID-19 pandemic in 2020, La Morada provided 2,500 meals a week—and often more—to our neighbors in need. The restaurant also offered employment to adults and students and served as a community center.

We read, beginning in Genesis 37, that the Hebrew patriarch Jacob loses sight of his twelve sons one day. Eleven of the sons manage to sell their brother, Joseph, to a caravan of merchants, who in turn sell him to the captain of Pharaoh's guard, Potiphar. Joseph is seduced by Potiphar's wife but refuses, and then he is accused of rape and imprisoned. In true Hamiltonian fashion, he survives it all and rises to nobility. Successfully using his gift to interpret dreams, he warns Pharaoh of a coming famine and wins his freedom. Eventually his brothers face starvation and seek refuge in him: the right hand of Pharaoh.

The family reunification, however, doesn't go smoothly. As an undocumented immigrant and asylum seeker, I read this cumbersome part of the story as part of the bureaucratic web of negotiations that one must navigate. There's always an elaborate process.

Joseph must feel compelled to provide for his struggling family. He must feel resentment and hurt. Ultimately, he must be careful not to jeopardize his vizier position. Upon reconnecting with his father, Jacob tells Joseph: "Now I am ready to die, since I have seen for myself that you are still alive" (Genesis 46:30). And upon facing Pharaoh, the supreme ruler of the land, Jacob says, "The years of my pilgrimage are a hundred and thirty. My years have been few and difficult, and they do not equal the years of the pilgrimage of my fathers" (Genesis 47:9).

Jacob knows everything depends on his visa interview with the Pharaoh. He knows that for his family's caravan of seventy to gain acceptance, he must articulate his pain and convince the ruler to give his family safe passage. Years of dreaming, sojourning, diplomacy, and exile have aged Jacob's soul and allowed him to empathize with the legacy that preceded him. He knows how his grandfather Abraham abandoned his hometown of Ur to follow a dream; how his father, Isaac, was almost sacrificed like a lamb, and how he stole the blessing of birthright and fled. The years have added up.

But unlike Jacob's reunification with Esau a generation earlier, during which Jacob had to surrender his riches, this time Jacob is greeted by Egyptians with mighty wealth. The Egyptians, through Joseph's work, give the family the best land as well as food according to the number of their children.

How do we greet the refugee and the asylum seeker today? Our current policies pale in comparison to the generosity of the Egyptians! The Egyptians were facing their own blight and scarcity; still, they chose not to turn to jingoism and scapegoating.

So how do you survive a famine? A pandemic? Perhaps you sell yourself out or sell out others, as Joseph's brothers did. Or perhaps you present the best version of yourself by feeding others, like my parents have done. You reconcile, you remember, you forgive, and you hope against hope. You pray that if you survive it, your descendants will do justice to your story so that they may survive theirs.

— REFLECT —

A generation after the death of Joseph, the Egyptians grew jealous of the prosperity of the Israelites and enslaved them. Again the cycle of exile, conflict, diplomacy, and sojourning repeated itself. The next agent of liberation was Moses, who similarly was trained in Pharaoh's palace and chose to identify with his oppressed heritage to lead his people to freedom. Where else in the Bible do you see the tension between displacement and reconciliation? How do you hear this in the Black spiritual "Let us cheer the weary traveler along the heavenly way"?

— READ —

Philippians 2:6–8. How was Joseph not beholden to the privileges of the palace? In what ways was he a precursor to Jesus's model of emptying himself of power?

— PRAY —

God who cries out with all creation for reconciliation and redemption, lead us away from separation and toward beloved community. You who continually show us how to empty ourselves of power, guide us to use our privilege to feed the hungry, return the exiled, and liberate the prisoner, until your kingdom come. Amen.

53

WE WHO ARE BECOMING

Noam Sandweiss-Back

"It is not light that we need, but fire; it is not the gentle shower, but thunder. We need the storm, the whirlwind, and the earthquake."

—FREDERICK DOUGLASS

READ: EXODUS 3

The shepherd wanders far into the wilderness. Through the rust-colored granite, the sun casts a slanting glow. The mountain brush looks ablaze. He walks farther and is startled to discover that this is no trick of the light—a bush is burning. He looks closer. The flames are crackling, and yet the bush is unconsumed.

He hears his name: Moses. He calls back with a question, and a voice answers: I am the God of your ancestors. I know the pain of your people, those now held in bondage. I've come to deliver them to freedom. You will help.

Moses is hesitant. He pushes back, equivocates. Finally, overwhelmed, he asks what he should say when his people demand the name of this God.

In English, God's response is often translated as "I Am Who I Am." But the Hebrew declares something else entirely: *Ehyeh Asher Ehyeh*. "I Will Be What I Will Be."

Moses then returns to slaveholding Egypt with a simple and explosive message for his people: I Will Be What I Will Be has sent for your liberation.

The mysterious truth of this name gets clearer with each day. Moses is awakened. He becomes a speech maker, organizer, militant. A whisper of dissent turns into a movement that swells across the enslaved multitude. Plagues of hunger, sickness, and death strangle the soul-sick society of the Egyptian Empire, and the Israelites discover an urgent and sacred call to be free. As they begin to take action together, and as the promise of emancipation blooms, God emerges through them.

God's presence expands as their action intensifies, and they are emboldened through this renewed relationship with the divine. After much struggle, they make a break for freedom and arrive at the shores of a great sea: an impassable expanse ahead and only death behind. They are trapped. The rabbinical commentary teaches that as the prospect of escape dwindles, one among them, an elder, walks into the sea until the salty water nearly fills his nostrils. Only then, on the edge of the man's last breath, does God split the waters.

Here is the truth of the name: God becomes as the people—poor, dispossessed, divided—become. God will be as the people will be. When the people find their voice, when they begin to unite and fight for their lives, God's voice echoes thunderously. Listen, God tells them. I will lead you out of Egypt.

Today we live in another kind of Egypt. The plagues of our day are poverty and precarity, hunger and homelessness, deep prejudice and hate. They are worsened by pandemics, not caused by them. In the richest country in history, we have been robbed of what should be universal rights to health, safety, and the fruits of our labor, and we have been dispossessed of the power to make it otherwise.

Did others before Moses stumble on the burning bush, see only a desert fire during the dry season, and move on? Is that not the same for so many of us today? We see the fire as fire and nothing more. We continue to march through the wilderness and toil in the shadow of empire, possessed by the belief that nothing can fundamentally change, that this is the best we can do.

But some stop and look closer. Some, out of necessity, are pulled toward the flames. These people recognize that within their communities— abandoned by the government and the wealthy—there is a spark, not only of combustion but of deep transformation.

These are the Moseses of our time. They are the fast-food workers fighting for living wages and a union, the tenants leading rent strikes, the unemployed pulling together organizing councils, the water protectors, and so many more. Like Moses, they are orphaned, disabled, homeless, refugees, and the leading edge of hope and new vision for us all. And just like that ancient prophet, they see a burning bush in every corner of this nation and hear their name called. They turn toward the ruling class to demand not small reforms but a complete reconstruction of society around the needs of all people.

When the Israelites arrive on the other side of the sea, it is no coincidence that they go to the mountain of the burning bush. They arrive on its dusty slopes to begin a new covenant with God and construct a social order founded on justice.

Perhaps, while camping there, they again see a bush on fire and glimpse within it their own becoming. Perhaps they hear a voice reminding them that the kind of revolutionary action they have taken has always been synonymous with the very name of God.

— REFLECT —

What do the burning bush and the story of Exodus teach us about our current time? How do you see God's "becoming" in today's struggle for justice? How do you understand your own becoming?

— READ —

1 Samuel 2:1-11. Through her song, Hannah offers a vision of who God is and of what God will become and will do for the poor.

— PRAY —

May we see that the miracle of the divine is the miracle of ourselves. May we become who we are meant to be. May we speak with the voice and name of all creation through our fight for freedom. Amen.

ACKNOWLEDGMENTS

We Cry Justice is an outgrowth of the Reading the Bible with the Poor Collaborative Inquiry project funded by Louisville Institute. This collaborative inquiry project brings together leaders from the Kairos Center, one of the anchor organizations of the Poor People's Campaign: A National Call for Moral Revival, who are poor and dispossessed, faith leaders, biblical scholars, and activists. Together we develop and utilize a method of contextual, liberative biblical interpretation and application to shift and shape Christianity's narrative and actions about poverty. We are grateful for Louisville Institute's support of this work to affect change in Christianity in North America.

This project would not be possible without the commitment and hard work of a large team of editors from the Reading the Bible with the Poor cohort who led this effort. We collectivized the planning and writing of this project by forming a team to guide the work and by pairing each author with a peer as a conversation partner in writing each entry. Thanks to Noam Sandweiss-Back, Solita Alexander Riley, Moses Hernandez McGavin, Dan Jones, Jessica C. Williams, and so many of the contributors to this book who read drafts and helped in other ways. Particular thanks are owed to Colleen Wessel-McCoy, who guided the project and the team of editors.

Special thanks and appreciation to our editor, Valerie Weaver-Zercher, and everyone at Broadleaf Books. We came to Valerie with a vision for the book, and she believed in that vision, built on it, and gave the book shape. Deep love and gratitude to Rev. Dr. William Barber II for the foreword and his vision and leadership of the Poor People's Campaign: A National Call for Moral Revival.

We acknowledge with thanksgiving the many freedom fighters in whose footsteps we follow in this struggle for liberation. Each of these authors has been shaped and developed by leaders and mentors who have gone before us—a great cloud of witnesses who, together with the Holy Spirit, guide our feet as we run this race. We dedicate this work to the freedom fighters of today and to the generations to come. Let us struggle together to build a world in which everybody can thrive and enjoy abundant life.

CONTRIBUTORS

Tonny H. Algood serves as pastor at the United Methodist Inner City Mission in Mobile, Alabama. He is a trichair of the Alabama Poor People's Campaign, serves on the executive board of the National Union of the Homeless, and is part of the University of the Poor and Freedom Church of the Poor.

William J. Barber II, DMin, is the president and senior lecturer of Repairers of the Breach; cochair of the Poor People's Campaign: A National Call for Moral Revival; bishop with the Fellowship of Affirming Ministries; visiting professor at Union Theological Seminary; pastor of Greenleaf Christian Church, Disciples of Christ, in Goldsboro, North Carolina; architect of the Forward Together Moral Mondays Movement; and the author of four books and numerous articles.

Adam Barnes, PhD, is the director of the rights and religions program at the Kairos Center and colead of the National Faith Partners team for the Poor People's Campaign: A National Call for Moral Revival. He was born in Saint Louis, grew up in Colorado, and currently lives in New York City with his wife, Shailly, and their three kids.

Tejai Beulah, PhD, is a historian and spiritual director. She is assistant professor of church history, ethics, and Black church and African diaspora studies at Methodist Theological School in Ohio. She is currently at work on a monograph about the intersection of evangelical Christianity and the Black Power movement.

Idalin Luz Montes Bobé is an educator, movement technologist, and organizer originally from Philadelphia. She has lived in cities across the United States and is currently based in Harlem. She cofounded the Popular Education Project in 2015 after being inspired by the Ferguson uprising and understanding she needed political education as part of her civic duty. She is active in the Poor People's Campaign: A National Call for Moral Revival and the University of the Poor.

Janelle Bruce is founding pastor of the Church Without Walls, Global Reach, with a vision to impact, inspire, and heal our communities through God's love. She was also an attorney organizer with Repairers of the Breach and the Poor People's Campaign: A National Call for Moral Revival. Her ministry is guided by Micah 6:8: do justice, love kindness, and walk humbly with God.

Keith M. Bullard II is a coordinator of Raise Up for $15 and Fight for $15 and a Union. He is a member of the Freedom Church of the Poor and has organized with national and local organizations such as the Poor People's Campaign: A National Call for Moral Revival, Movement for Black Lives, Durham Workers Assembly, Black Workers for Justice, and others. Bullard is originally from Inkster, Michigan, and now resides in Durham, North Carolina, with his loving wife, Crystal, and their three children.

Claire Chadwick is a licensed American Baptist minister living in Kansas. She is also an essential and low-wage worker. She has testified nationally and served as a Kansas trichair as part of the Poor People's Campaign: A National Call for Moral Revival. She is part of the Nonviolent Medicaid Army and a regular preacher at Freedom Church of the Poor. Chadwick has a master of divinity degree and a degree in counseling.

C. Wess Daniels, PhD, is the William R. Rogers director of Friends Center and Quaker Studies at Guilford College and a Quaker minister. He lives in Greensboro, North Carolina, with his wife, Emily, and their three children. Daniels's recent publications include *Resisting Empire* and *A Convergent Model of Renewal*.

Becca Forsyth is a leader with the Poor People's Campaign: A National Call for Moral Revival at the local, state, and national levels. She currently serves as a trichair of the New York State Poor People's Campaign. She recently earned her master's in social work from Rutgers University while also being the primary caregiver for her disabled husband. Forsyth is a proud daughter, sister, wife, mother, and grandmother.

Carolyn Jean Foster was born, raised, and educated in Birmingham, Alabama. She is a deacon at Saint Mark's Episcopal Church and cochair of the Commission on Truth, Justice and Racial Reconciliation for the Episcopal Diocese of Alabama. She has served as executive director of the Alabama Faith Council and is currently Faith in Community coordinator of Greater Birmingham Ministries. She is also serving as trichair for the Alabama Poor People's Campaign: A National Call for Moral Revival.

Letiah Fraser is a New York City native who now lives in Kansas City. She is an ordained pastor in the Church of the Nazarene. Fraser is an organizer connected with the Kansas Poor People's Campaign, a disability rights activist, a hospital chaplain, and a doctoral student. She has degrees from Nyack College and Nazarene Theological Seminary and is currently completing a doctorate of ministry at Nazarene Theological Seminary. Her focus is on spiritual formation and disability theology.

Karenna Gore is the founder and director of the Center for Earth Ethics at Union Theological Seminary. She has also worked as a lawyer, a writer, and director of community relations for the Association to Benefit Children. Gore grew up in northern Virginia and middle Tennessee and now lives in New York City.

Charon Hribar, PhD, is the director of cultural strategies at the Kairos Center for Religions, Rights, and Social Justice and the codirector of cultural arts for the Poor People's Campaign: A National Call for Moral Revival. Over the past sixteen years, Hribar has been dedicated to the work of political education, leadership development, and integrating the use of arts and culture for movement building with community and religious leaders across the country.

Daniel Jones is an educator and organizer based in Miami, Florida. He is part of the University of the Poor, the Freedom Church of the Poor, the Poor People's Campaign: A National Call for Moral Revival, the Popular Education Project, and Put People First! PA. His research and writing focus on the roots of Jewish traditions of justice in the historical freedom struggles of the ancient Israelites and their meaning for us today.

Brigitte Kahl is professor of New Testament and Bible at Union Theological Seminary in New York and an ordained minister of the Protestant Church of Berlin-Brandenburg. A native of East Germany, she studied and taught at Humboldt University of Berlin until 1997. She reads the Bible empire-critically as a book of resilience, resistance, and liberation, with a specific focus on Genesis, Luke, and Paul. Poverty, social injustice, racism, sexism, and ecoimperialism are major topics of her work.

Nicholas Laccetti served as the communications director for the Kairos Center. He began his work at Kairos as a Poverty Initiative fellow in 2013. He is the author of *The Inner Church Is the Hope of the World*. Laccetti holds a master's in medieval studies from Fordham University and a master of divinity degree from Union Theological Seminary. He is based in New York City.

Savina J. Martin, DHL, is a poverty scholar and US Army veteran whose focus is mobilizing and studying the social and economic effects of systemic poverty. She is an advisor with the National Union of the Homeless and sits on its Clergy Council. She is currently an instructor with the University of the Poor Homeless Union History Project and a trichair of the Massachusetts Poor People's Campaign: A National Call for Moral Revival. Martin is from Massachusetts.

Sarah Monroe is cofounder and director of Chaplains on the Harbor and Harbor Roots Farm, organizations that raise up the leadership of poor people in Grays Harbor County, Washington. She holds a master of divinity degree from Episcopal Divinity School. She is a farmer and Episcopal priest who loves to explore the Olympic Peninsula.

Melanie Mullen serves as the Episcopal Church's director of reconciliation, justice, and creation care. Before joining the presiding bishop's staff, she was the downtown missioner in Richmond, Virginia, bringing fifteen years of campaign fundraising and nonprofit experience to justice and reconciliation ministry in the urban South. She received a master of divinity degree from Virginia Theological Seminary and has studied at the University of North Carolina and Clark Atlanta University.

Stephen Pavey, PhD, is founder of Hope In Focus. He is a contemplative activist, photographer, writer, and witness. His publications include *Eclipse of Dreams, Make Holy the Bare Life*, and *Theologies of Power and Crisis*. He lives in Lexington, Kentucky.

Michael Pollack grew up in Rockville, Maryland. During his last year of rabbinical school in Philadelphia, he cofounded March on Harrisburg, a group dedicated to making corruption illegal by passing anticorruption, pro-democracy bills in Pennsylvania. Rabbi Pollack lives in Philadelphia, and his hobbies include convincing politicians to not be corrupt, long marches through the Pennsylvania countryside, and sitting down in inconvenient places in the state capitol.

Solita Alexander Riley is committed to ending poverty. She has served as educator and family counselor and is now most grateful to continue the struggle through Kairos Center membership. Riley serves as a prayer warrior and budding theologian with the Freedom Church of the Poor and moonlights in municipal government. She holds degrees from Harvard University, Columbia University, and Union Theological Seminary. Born in Belize to a proud Guyanese family, Riley now lives in Harlem with her husband and son.

Tammy Rojas resides in Lancaster, Pennsylvania, and is a coordinator in Put People First! PA, a statewide organization fighting for health care as a human right. She organizes closely with the National Union of the Homeless and is a member of the coordinating committee of the Pennsylvania Poor People's Campaign. She has authored articles that include "The Price the Poor Pay for Gentrification: The Ewell Plaza Development" and "Save Our Hospitals! The Fight to Put People over Profits."

 **Marco Saavedra** has lived as an undocumented immigrant for twenty-seven years and is currently seeking political asylum stemming from his immigrant justice work. He works at his family's Oaxacan restaurant, La Morada, in the South Bronx, and enjoys painting and exploring the Hudson Valley with his baby niece. He is coauthor of *Shadows Then Light* and *Eclipse of Dreams*, and his activism is featured in *The Infiltrators*.

 **Noam Sandweiss-Back** is an organizer and writer born in Jerusalem and raised in New Jersey. He is the director of partnerships for the Poor People's Campaign: A National Call for Moral Revival and the program manager for the Kairos Center for Religions, Rights, and Social Justice. During the COVID-19 pandemic, he moved back to his hometown in northern New Jersey.

 **Aaron Scott** is the cofounder of Chaplains on the Harbor. He is the missioner for antipoverty organizing in the Episcopal Diocese of Olympia and serves on the national steering committee of the Poor People's Campaign: A National Call for Moral Revival. Scott is also the proud dad of Moses.

 **Liz Theoharis**, PhD, is founder and director of the Kairos Center for Religions, Rights, and Social Justice at Union Theological Seminary and cochair of the Poor People's Campaign: A National Call for Moral Revival alongside Bishop William J. Barber II. She has spent more than two decades organizing among the poor in the United States, working with and advising grassroots organizations. She is a professor, biblical scholar, and pastor in the Presbyterian Church (USA). Theoharis lives with her husband and two children in New York City.

Kenia Torres-Alcocer is an organizer with Union de Vecinos and a leader in the Los Angeles Tenants Union. She has been working with Union de Vecinos since 2003, when she was eighteen years old, organizing neighborhood committees in Boyle Heights and the city of Maywood. An undocumented mother of two, Torres-Alcocer is also a member of the Popular Education Project and has served as trichair of the California Poor People's Campaign and as a steering committee member of the Poor People's Campaign: A National Call for Moral Revival.

Leonardo Vilchis was born and raised in Mexico. He has lived and worked in the Los Angeles Boyle Heights neighborhood for the last thirty-four years and learned to read the Bible with members of church-based communities in the Pico-Aliso housing projects, the largest public housing development west of the Mississippi. He is a cofounder of the Union de Vecinos in Boyle Heights and the Los Angeles Tenants Union.

Colleen Wessel-McCoy, PhD, has taught at Arizona State University and Union Theological Seminary and is the author of *Freedom Church of the Poor*. Originally from Marietta, Georgia, Colleen was cocoordinator of poverty scholarship and leadership development at the Kairos Center and colead of the Moral Fusion Student Organizing Fellowship of the Poor People's Campaign: A National Call for Moral Revival and is part of the Clergy Council of the National Union of the Homeless.

Erica N. Williams is an international human rights activist. She is the founding pastor of Set It Off Ministries and a national social justice organizer for Repairers of the Breach and the Poor People's Campaign: A National Call for Moral Revival. Williams is a member of the Freedom Church of the Poor, the Popular Education Project, and Black Christians for Palestine and a trustee for the World Student Christian Federation. She is ordained in the Christian Church (Disciples of

Christ). Rev. Erica's life mission is summed up in the social gospel passage of Luke 4:18–19. She is a native of Saginaw, Michigan.

Jessica C. Williams was a founding member of the Poverty Initiative at the Kairos Center for Religions, Rights, and Social Justice and is one of the leaders within the Kansas Poor People's Campaign: A National Call for Moral Revival. She has pastored American Baptist churches in New York, Iowa, and Kansas and currently serves as director of alumni engagement and lifelong learning at Central Baptist Theological Seminary in Shawnee, Kansas.

Clinton Wright is a national social justice organizer with Repairers of the Breach, a member of the national field team with the Poor People's Campaign: A National Call for Moral Revival, a member of the core team of Fed Up Food Distribution, an educator with the University of the Poor, and a deacon with the Freedom Church of the Poor. He is based in Durham, North Carolina.